SON OF A JUNKMAN...
My Life from the West Bottoms of Kansas City to Hollywood

ED ASNER
with SAMUEL WARREN JOSEPH and MATTHEW SEYMOUR

Copyright © 2019, Ed Asner

Cover design by Leonard Kenyon and Matthew Seymour

ISBN: 978-0-9600871-0-5 (hardcover)

ISBN: 978-0-9600871-1-2 (softcover)

Library of Congress Control Number: 2019901772

All Rights Reserved. No part of this book may be reproduced or transmitted in any form or by any means, electronic or mechanical, including photocopying, recording, or by any information storage and retrieval system without written permission from the author, except for the inclusion of brief quotations in a review.

Printed in the United States of America.

For my family—
Nancy, Matt, Liza, Katie, and Charlie

CONTENTS●●●

Foreword by Paul Rudd ix
Introduction xiii

1. JEWS IN THE BOTTOMS 1
2. MOVIN' ON UP 7
3. TO PLAY OR NOT TO PLAY 15
4. GOODBYE COLLEGE, HELLO REAL WORLD 18
5. THE FRENCH CONNECTION 24
6. A BUNCH OF COMMIES 28
7. PURSUING THE TRUTH 36
8. HOLLYWOOD HUSTLE 41
9. OH, MR. GRANT 51
10. CAN ED ASNER DO DRAMA? 59
11. "THE JANE FONDA OF LATIN AMERICA" 64
12. ROCK BOTTOM 75
13. PICKING MYSELF *UP* 80
14. ODE TO THE JUNKMAN 91

Afterword by Samuel Warren Joseph................................ 95
Additional Interviews 97
Acknowledgments 139
Notes 142

SON OF A
JUNKMAN

FOREWORD •••

When Ed calls me on the phone, I *Asner*.

That might be the worst joke ever to start a foreword but be forewarned: I have never written a foreword before. I really don't know how to do this properly. In fact, as I'm typing this, I'm going to ask Google the best way to write one. Hold on a sec…

Okay, I'm back. Wow. There are a lot of people out there who think they have a handle on the best way to do it. Forget it, I'm going on instinct. By definition, a foreword is an introduction to a book, but as Ed is someone I love and respect, I'd rather introduce you to the guy I know—the one whom you'll learn a bit more about on these next hundred or so pages.

"Call me back you Jew bastard!" I've received this voice mail several times from Ed over the years when I didn't *Asner* the phone. It always makes me giggle. Minus the seven Emmys he's won and a whole bunch of other things, Ed's and my stories share a unique similarity.

We're both Jewish actors of Eastern European descent who grew up in Kansas City. That's a fairly small cross section. On the Venn diagram, Ed and I may be the only two in the middle. There's an argument for Mandy Patinkin, but he grew up in Chicago and only *attended* the University of Kansas as an undergrad. Not bad, but technically that just gets you an honorable mention.

When you're from Kansas City, you grow up knowing Ed Asner is hometown royalty. I'd always hoped to meet him, and in 2012 it finally happened. That year I was fortunate enough to be cast in the Broadway play *Grace* starring three wonderful actors—Michael Shannon, Kate Arrington, and a strapping, young Edward Mordechai Asner. Full disclosure, I have no idea if that's Ed's middle name. In fact, I'm sure it isn't because I just made it up. Back to Google. Hold on another sec…

The first thing I noticed about Yitzhak Edward Asner is that he doesn't hold back from how he feels about anything. First rehearsals are a bit like the first day of school. There's a reservation as everyone meets everyone else and gets a lay of the land. Not with Ed. He burst in the room like a tornado of jokes and complaints about how "HOLY F***ING HOT!!!" it was outside. He's opinionated, gruff, and outspoken. But—and this is his magic trick—always with a twinkle in his eye.

He's the kind of guy who can call you a "Jew bastard" and make it feel like a compliment because you know that it is. I took a shine to him immediately. He's just so damn funny. The misnomer is curmudgeon. Actual curmudgeons are grumps and Ed is the opposite. He has a heart of gold. Personally, I think he loves to play up the grumpiness, but what I got right off the bat is that Ed Asner is a 100 percent gooey-in-the-middle total and complete softie. You have to be to play Santa Claus, right? And let's face it, he's the best Santa to ever play the part. Not bad for a Jew from the Midwest.

As a young boy in Kansas City he said he "felt like an outsider from the other side." That feeling of not belonging followed him throughout his life. Perhaps that's why he's so empathetic to those less fortunate than himself—those on the outside. He's always fought for those whose voices have trouble being heard. I knew this about Ed as I'd heard about his work with autism before I met him. I also knew he was previously the president of the Screen Actors Guild for many years. But there was so much I didn't know, and reading the book I got to know so much more.

It hasn't always been easy for him—in the book he delves into the time he was blackballed from the industry he loved for taking a political stand. His reaction to these events is gripping. His admission of guilt over his failed marriage is brutally honest and must have been difficult for him to write, but Ed has never been afraid to speak the truth, no matter the cost. His willingness to appear fallible and even broken pulls us in close. Like all of us, he is undeniably human.

He's also had an undeniably remarkable career. How many people can claim they played the *same* character on TV in two *completely different* genres both equally iconic? Ed resides in the space all actors dream of working—someone who's just as convincing playing someone hateful as he is someone gentle and kind. It is a serious skill and requires a deftness that's easy to take for granted. Rather, to take for *Lou Granted*. Again, I apologize. It had been way too long since I told a clunker of a joke and I didn't like the way it felt.

Family. Friends. Foes. All of those words start with the letter *F*, but you probably guessed that or at least went back and checked. I know more about Ed's family, friends, and foes from having read this book and it makes me feel closer to him. Whether working with John Wayne or Elvis Presley, crossing paths with Harpo Marx or Fidel Castro (unconfirmed, but read the book and judge for yourself) and so many others, Ed's journey has been a fascinating one. His is a life fully lived. *Son of a Junkman* is the culmination of that life and one I'm eternally grateful to have encountered in my own.

—Paul Rudd, *Grace* costar and fellow Kansas Citian

INTRODUCTION •••

As the title of this book suggests, I am the son of a junkman. My father owned Asner Iron & Steel, located at 34 North James in Kansas City, Kansas.

Many people hear the word *junk* and think *worthless*. They don't realize what a junkyard is or what a junkman does. A lot of people look down on those who work with junk. They visualize a junkman and see someone who is dirty and surrounded by stink lines, very Pepé Le Pew–like. I, myself, was guilty of this stereotype as a child.

I learned how to cope with living in the West Bottoms early in my life. I also adapted to being a Jew in Kansas City because it was something I couldn't change. The thing that was the most difficult for me was being the son of a junkman.

I was embarrassed of what my father did for a living. My brothers and sisters would even prepare me on how to answer that recurring question, "What does your father do?"

"Uh, he deals with used materials."

"He sells reclaimed items."

"He's a professional recycler."

I used every lie imaginable to hide my dad's profession. It wasn't until I was a few years older that I realized what my father really did. And, boy, did I see him in a new light.

There are many misconceptions about being a junkman. One being that a junkyard is simply filled with garbage, overflowing with rats and cockroaches. That, however, is more like a landfill, not a junkyard.

Merriam-Webster's Unabridged Dictionary defines *junkman* as "a person who deals in resalable junk." Okay, but what is *junk* exactly?

The dictionary has many definitions for the word *junk*. One is "something of poor quality," which it connects to the word *trash*. No, that's not it.

Another definition is "something of little meaning, worth, or significance." Nope, that's still not it.

A third definition is "old iron, glass, paper, or other waste that may be used again in some form" or "secondhand, worn, or discarded articles."

Bingo!

There's an old saying: *One man's junk is another man's treasure.* This phrase likely doesn't have much meaning to my readers, but it means something to me.

My father dealt with everything under the sun. He sold:

- Metals, including brass, copper, lead, tin, iron, aluminum, you name it.
- Paper goods, including books, newsprint, magazines, and cardboard.
- Glass bottles of all shapes, sizes, and colors.
- Fabrics, including cotton, silk, wool, and mohair.
- Bones, yes, *actual* bones. I still don't know who bought them or for what reason. On second thought, I don't want to know.

My dad always saw value in these items and materials. One time he bought a truckload of old books from a farm and among them was an 1850s edition of Homer's *Odyssey*. He also found elaborate archival books in Spanish. He introduced me to worlds and adventures I might never have come across if not for his profession.

Another misunderstanding about owning a junkyard is that it can't be profitable. However, I was always one of the better-off kids in my school. I was never hungry or left wanting. I was given endless opportunities, even with four siblings, because of that junkyard and the junkman who owned it.

My father's junkyard is still in business today. My brother took over the family business, along with his son-in-law. I have been told that it is the oldest Jewish-owned business in Greater Kansas City. So, as you can see, dealing junk can be very profitable.

If I had to define what a *junkman* means to me, the *Ed Asner Dictionary* would define it as "a hard-working individual who provides for his family" or "a business-savvy person who sees value when others don't."

This book is about my life, which I owe to a junkman and a junkyard. Hopefully, after you read this book, you will have newfound respect for that good ol' hardworking junkman in your neighborhood.

This one's for you, Pops.

CHAPTER 1
JEWS IN THE BOTTOMS

"How could I ever become something? My mom, dad, and four siblings were hard acts to follow."

I was born in Evangelical Hospital in Kansas City, Missouri, on November 15, 1929. Evidently, there wasn't a hospital room available on the Kansas side, which was very primitive at the time, so I was born in a Missouri hospital. I was raised, however, in the West Bottoms of Kansas City, Kansas, across from the Armour Packing Company.

My mother, Lizzie, or "Momma" as I call her, came to America from Russia with her family in 1913; this included her father, sisters, and her two brothers, Morris and Frank; Frank was a brawler and a street fighter.

Almost all of them, including the women, worked in a packing house, along with my grandfather. The women stayed there about a year each, until they got married or enough of a stake to take on something more substantial.

My mother was certainly well along in her forties when she had me. She was 82 when she died in 1967. I remember her fondly. She always had nothing but love and kind words for me.

She was a strong woman who never complained about taking care of her family. She would always clean the house and fix dinner for my father and siblings. She was the type of woman that at the end of each meal would eat whatever she could scrape off the other plates. This was not because we were needy but because she couldn't stand to see food go to waste.

My mother was an impressive woman who could do it all. One memory I have of her is when we went to picnics at the temple. Mom would always win the nail-pounding contest. That must be where I get my strong and muscular arms from.

During the war when all my older siblings were either in the service or away from home, my mother would go with my father to the junkyard he owned. She would wear her pumps while working there. One day, she was pushing a wheelbarrow and stepped on a meat hook, which went through the top of her foot. I still vividly remember her limping around the house with a bandaged foot. Even though I'm sure she was in great pain, she never complained.

That was my momma.

My father came to America from the village of Nacha, outside Eishyshok, Lithuania, in the late 1890s. He was a man whose physicality I feared, but he never laid a finger on me. His hands were twice as wide as mine. I used to marvel at him taking a cigarette, knocking the ash off, and how his hands were nothing but callouses.

Everybody would say, "Don't tell your father, don't let your father know. Don't do this, don't do that." In doing so, they built a wall around him that I dared not cross. This was not based on what *he* said to me, but everyone else's warnings.

My father met my mother at the invitation of my grandfather. It was all horse and wagons at the time and my mother didn't think my dad was very impressive. He didn't have much money and was sleeping with his dog down in the West Bottoms. I think she envisioned that her main job would be picking fleas off my father.

However, my grandfather took the reins and wrote my father a message saying, "I just want you to know, we want you, we welcome you, please come back." With my grandfather's persistence, my mother eventually warmed up to him. After dating for less than a year, my parents decided to marry on Christmas Day.

My father was a tough guy. A couple of years ago my brother told me a story about him. As the story goes, my grandfather lived on the Missouri side, and come Pesach, he'd make wine. I don't know if he sold it, but evidently prohibition was in effect. Supposedly, one of his neighbors found out he was making the wine, so he approached my grandfather and said, "You gotta give me some money so I don't squeal."

What a handsome couple, my mom and dad. Can you see where I get my good looks?
Courtesy of Asner Family Photo Collection

Well, my grandfather was terror stricken, he couldn't believe it. He was a scholar, a Yiddish scholar. So, he told my mother, she told my father, and my father said, "Don't worry. I'll take care of it."

I never knew my father to be a brawler, but evidently come the next morning at dawn, my dad got in his car and drove to the Missouri side. He parked around the corner, walked to my grandfather's house, and told him to lay low, he'd "handle it."

So, the neighbor came by sometime later, knocked on the screen door.

"Hey, *Seliger!*" he yelled my grandfather's name, pronouncing it, "Sellicker."

"You got my money?"

"Come on in," my dad mumbled.

When he entered the house, my father beat the shit out of him. My dad then, in his best cowboy impression, said, "Is that enough money for ya?"

My grandfather never heard from the neighbor again.

Another interesting story about my father came during my college days. He ran a junkyard and, at one point, he started making stills during prohibition. In Kansas City, Italians were profiting from bootlegging, in terms of big money. So Dad, being the enterprising soul that he was, being a junkman, could lay claim to lots of sheet copper. Well, sheet copper is essential for stills. My dad came across a man named Brock who knew how to make stills. So, the junkyard would be open during the day and Brock would come at night to make stills. My father either sold them or rented them throughout the various areas of the city.

One time, I ran into a cop on a streetcar when I was home from college. I began talking to him, and he said he knew my father. He was talking about one particular raid where they found a thousand-gallon still. He said they punched a few holes in it, took it down to city hall, and put it up for auction. As usual, my father, the junkman, would come down, buy his still back for pennies, and then sell it again.

That was my father.

●○●●○●●○●●○

My parents didn't intend to have me. My dad was busy in El Dorado, Arkansas, losing a fortune. He was exchanging letters with my mother at the time. However, my father didn't know how to read English, so the letters had to be read to him. My parents agreed that if my mother was pregnant, she'd make a *puntilla*, a mark, on the letter. So, after someone would read each letter to my father, he would ask, "Is there a mark?" That's how he found out she was pregnant with me.

I had four older siblings. My oldest sibling, Ben, was born in January 1915. He was a chubby kid who was picked on a lot by others. Because of the constant teasing, Ben grew tough and used his weight to his advantage. He ended up with a V-shaped body. Ben couldn't have been taller than 5'9", but he certainly was the strongest of the boys in the family. He was average height but broad and strong.

Due to our age difference and a run-in with the law, Ben was not at home very often when I was growing up. I never saw much of him because he was out in the world. He did not go to college, but he was good at math and a salesman type.

When we had father-son outings at the temple, Ben would wrestle for the sporting events. Sometimes I wonder, what schmuck would dare to challenge him? Must have been the dummy of the crowd.

My sister Eve was the second oldest. She was born in April 1916. Actually, her name began with an *R*, but Ben couldn't pronounce it so his fracturing of her name turned into Eve. Since I was the baby of the family, Eve would pick out my wardrobe and change my diapers.

Eve worked as a social worker for a Jewish welfare organization in Kansas City for a while. She went to Washington University in St. Louis. After moving back to Kansas City for a short time, she became an assistant buyer at the department store Stix Baer & Fuller in St. Louis.

She was regarded as the beauty of the family. There was a time when she was involved with a guy, but my father refused to let the courtship continue after he found out the man was divorced.

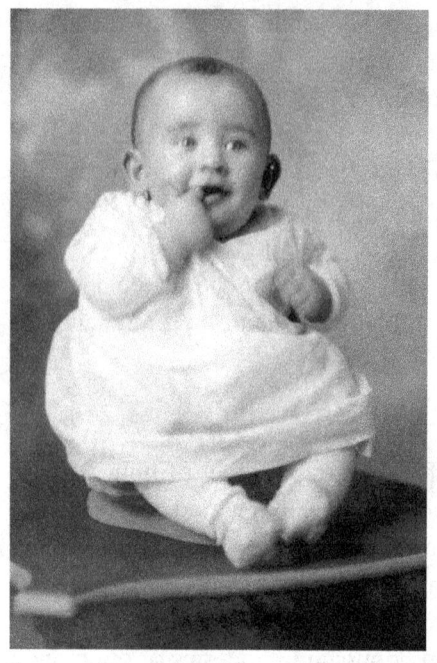

Some things never change...except my diapers are no longer cloth.
Courtesy of Asner Family Photo Collection

After Eve came my sister Esther. She was born in May 1919. She was a tomboy. She proved to be an invaluable sibling to me during the war years. I leaned on her a lot. Esther would come home and type my applications for college. She was a lonely woman who worked for a Naval Aviation Photographic Unit in Kodiak, Alaska, during the war. She fell in love with a man from Alaska but gave that up because he wasn't Jewish, so she would lean on me for emotional support.

One time, I remember coming home with Esther and my brother Labe. She said, "The car needs water." I said, "Okay," got up, grabbed the hose, and put water in the gas tank. When Esther found out, she slapped me. She was a joy to be around.

In May 1923, my second brother, Labe, was born. He was six and a half years older than me. Even though Labe was short, he overcame his shortness by being feisty. He loved to pinch me to the point that my skin would bruise. I always likened him to be the *Ulysses* of the family, always plotting.

Labe was the only one dumb enough to challenge my brother Ben. Once, Ben wouldn't surrender the Ping-Pong table and Labe thought it was wise to confront him. He quickly learned his lesson.

Labe died a year ago. God, I miss him.

My beautiful sister, Eve.
Courtesy of Asner Family Photo Collection

What a beautiful family. I'm that future Casanova in the middle.
Courtesy of Asner Family Photo Collection

My family meant the world to me. I was so proud that this noble line had dribbled out into me. When it came time for the high holidays and we went to the temple, I thought we had the best-looking men and prettiest women in the whole synagogue.

To me, I was the schlub who brought up the tail end. I remember feeling daunted and thinking, *How could I ever become something flying into that opposition?* My mom, dad, and four siblings were hard acts to follow. I miss them all.

CHAPTER 2...
MOVIN' ON UP

"Looking back, at that young age, I think it was better that I was kept in the dark."

My earliest memory was the sun of the Depression, the baking sun of the Depression, which drove lots of farmers off the ground...and seeing all the workers from the packing house on the streets in their white coats, splattered with blood.

And about a mile, or half mile, down the road was the covered passageway over which the Judas goats would lead the cattle and the sheep into the slaughterhouse. And I never thought about it then—most of the denizens of the West Bottoms (Kansas City) at that time, some living in my father's houses or shacks that he built, were a combination of Mexicans, some blacks, and the whites consisting mostly of what we termed *hunkies, bohunks*. My mother's family, when they came over in 1913, almost all of them, including the girls, worked in the packing house, including my grandfather. And they stayed there about, I suppose, a year each, until they got husbands or got enough of a stake to take on something more representative.

I remember one time a steer got loose from the herd and ended up in our yard. The poor thing was running around all nervous. Eventually, one of my parents picked me up and threw me in a shed until the steer could be

I still have the same teeth.
Courtesy of Asner Family Photo Collection

7

returned to the packing house. As an animal lover, the sight of this didn't affect me until a later age. How I ever ate meat again, I'll never know.

I grew up in the West Bottoms, an industrial area just south of the Missouri River. It was populated by nothing but stockyards, packing houses, and trucking companies. It was dry as toast. The only tree that could survive there was the ailanthus tree, also known as the "tree of heaven." It thrived off the dry, hard, and brittle soil found in the Bottoms. I would always call it the "Jewish tree" of the Bottoms because we thrived there while others couldn't.

I vividly remember the Kansas summers during my childhood. It was so hot that the firemen would turn the fire hydrants on and the neighborhood kids would run back and forth, in and out of the water. The water pressure was so strong that we were practically swept into the streets.

There was a time when my mom bought me new boxer shorts, with patterns and everything. I thought they were so beautiful that I begged and pleaded with her to let me wear them outside. She finally gave me permission and the whole entire neighborhood had a glimpse of me running through the fire hydrant water, getting wet with my boxer shorts clinging to my tuchus.

I started school in 1935. I attended kindergarten and first grade at Cooper School. My two chief companions were Tony and Boner, and yes, that was his real name, Boner Lombreno.

The three of us used to get in some kind of trouble. One cold day, we were out playing and we were all wearing long johns. I forget the reason, but we decided to take off our underwear. After playing, or whatever the hell we did, we put our underwear back on and went home.

"Why are your long johns so black?!" my mother yelled. "It's like you sat in coal dust!"

Then I realized, I had put on the wrong pair of underwear! Now, as I recall this story, I sure hope that was coal dust...

The principal of Cooper School was Mrs. Miller. She was jolly, warm, and caring. It's hard to tell, being in the slum section of the city, how much attention was paid to me since I was one of the better-off kids in the neighborhood.

There was a boy that would pick on me in the first grade. His name was Cindrich. He kept picking on me and picking on me. One day, my friend Tony told me, "You gotta stand up, man, you gotta stand up. You can't let him do that."

The next time he started picking on me, I stood up and said, "You can't do that, man!" He arched his brows and simply said, "Oh." He shut up and moved on. I thought, *That's wonderful. He left me alone.*

As time went on, he started doing it again. He got bolder and bolder and I became more and more frightened because I didn't know what I was going to do to protect myself again. Thankfully, my family moved before I had to make that decision.

When I was in the second grade, my sister Eve convinced my parents to move into an area called Westheight Manor, or what I like to call "White Bread Village."

It was a cleaned-up section of Kansas City, Kansas. It was quite a departure, leaving the dust, dirt, and blood in the Bottoms for the tall trees, fall foliage, and green grass of the new neighborhood.

We lived at 1814 Oakland Avenue. The street housed a few doctors and the managers of J. C. Penney and the local airport. Our house was made of brick and I was very proud of it.

One noted difference between the neighborhoods was the aura of Kansas City bigotry. The reason I call it White Bread Village is because there were no minorities.

When I grew up in the Bottoms, my two best friends, Tony and Boner, were Mexican. When I transferred to Mark Twain Grade School, I discovered a whole new world. There was not a single minority to be found. Being Jewish, I felt like an outsider from the other side. I felt like I didn't belong. This feeling followed me throughout my life.

Though I attended Hebrew school every day after regular school, taking the bus and a streetcar to get there, I was quite happy attending Mark Twain Grade School. I developed a strong bond with several classmates.

Dee Roy was my best friend. His father was the swim coach at Wyandotte High School. He lived three to four blocks from where I lived. I would always walk out of my way after school each day just to be with him and my friends.

After we moved, I had to share a bedroom with my brother Labe. I had to sleep with him and bear his jives, taunts, and goads, but I adored him. He was clever and a good athlete. I tipped the chart at around 5'9" when I was full grown. I would say his full height was 5'7". So, as good an athlete as he was, he'd bemoan the fact that he was so short and that he could never make it as a professional athlete. However, he was a devil in basketball, a good fielder, and I'm sure he was a good hitter.

One night, I remember, I traded a jackknife to get a "Tijuana bible," also called a two-by-four. If you don't know what that is, look it up or use your imagination. I was very proud of my procurement.

While lying in bed with Labe that night, he demanded to know why I was giggling. I showed him the bible and before I could stop him, he took it, and spent five minutes grumbling about how filthy it was that I possessed that kind of literature. He then ran to the bathroom and when he came out much later, the bible was missing.

I asked what he did with the bible and he said, "I tore it up and flushed it down the toilet." I felt ashamed, but then remembered what a liar he was. He loved to start trouble and put one over on me. I'm sure that bible got plenty of use while in his possession.

Even though my father never laid a hand on me, Labe was a different story. Every time he would harass and tease me, my mom would say, "If you don't stop that, I'm going to send Dad up." Of course, Labe, the bastard that he was, kept doing it. And, finally, you'd hear a chair moving back in the dining room, then you'd hear *boom, boom, boom,* the sound of my father coming upstairs. He would burst into our room where we slept and slap the shit out of Labe.

One time, my parents were out and we were home alone with our sister Eve. Labe was being a brat to me and she came upstairs and slapped him with her high-heeled shoe.

I was always protected by my family.

● ● ● ● ● ● ● ● ● ●

At Mark Twain Grade School, I found myself noticing girls more than ever before. That feeling followed me throughout my school days. At one point in the seventh grade, I became a crossing guard and took my duties very seriously.

I remember being highly insulted when my co-guard and I were accused of providing too much attention to these twin girls. I guess my Casanova charm started at a young age.

My first so-called crush came in the eighth grade. Dee Roy, my best friend, knew I liked a girl named Nancy. Dee Roy was a short guy, but the belle of the class, a girl named Marian, had a crush on him. However, Dee Roy was too intimidated and macho to act as if he was interested in her. Marian kept dogging him to take her out so Dee Roy said to me, "All right, you ask Nancy out, and I'll go on a double date with you."

So, I asked Nancy out but her parents refused. I wrote it off to the fact that they didn't want a Jewish kid taking their daughter out. I don't know if there is any truth to that, but that's how I felt at the time because I was the only Jewish kid in class.

Even though I was the only one, I never felt prejudice, but I felt the potential for prejudice. My family always talked about "anti-Semite this, anti-Semite that."

I'd also hear the phrase, "He'd Jew me down," outside of the house. I really didn't know what that meant at the time, but I figured it was deprecating.

I was blackballed by a fraternity in high school. My friend who was in the fraternity said, "I'm sorry they blackballed you." I said, "Was it because I was Jewish?" and he said, "Yeah." I was so relieved that it wasn't *me* who was blackballed but the *Jew*. What a putz!

I eventually joined a fraternity in my senior year. There was a boy a year older than me, a Jewish kid, who was in the fraternity before me. He was popular and well liked. So, I'd go to the fraternity meetings and they'd find some reason to dish out punishment. These little guys with paddles would paddle my tuchus. It was all for a laugh.

● ○ ● ○ ● ○ ● ○ ● ○

I stopped going to Hebrew school after my bar mitzvah, even though I still had an agreement with my rabbi. The contract said that I would continue to go to heder for a year after my bar mitzvah. Unfortunately, I didn't fulfill my end of the promise.

I don't have regrets about reneging on the agreement. I constantly went to Hebrew school, every day after regular school. My schoolmates were playing three-corner lot football and basketball while I was studying with my rabbi. I was denied that camaraderie because of Hebrew school.

While I was studying Hebrew, the rabbi decided that the younger kids would go four days a week to Hebrew school while the older kids would only go two days a week. This was because the rabbi knew he couldn't stop the older kids' complaining. By the time I was the oldest kid in the class, the rules were reversed. I still had to go four days a week! I looked around the classroom realizing I was royally screwed.

In my mind, I put the time in and learned Hebrew. I could swear that I had what was called a "five-thousand-word vocabulary" in Hebrew.

I remember, one day in class, I was very depressed and my rabbi asked me why I was sad. I said, "Well, my peers are out there playing basketball, and forging bonds, and I'm here segregated from them."

He tried to cheer me up about what a great student I was and how he had great confidence and hopes for me. I realized that it was a wasted effort. So, I continued looking forward to my bar mitzvah.

Sometime in the summer, the rabbi informed me that he was preparing me not only for the bar mitzvah, but that I was going to lead the Saturday morning service as well. He said I only had six weeks before my bar mitzvah to achieve the preparation. That scared the shit out of me.

So, I prepared. I learned the chants and the davening to lead the service. That means I would do my haftarah, the service, and my speech. It was a big load. I was twelve years old and in a constant state of terror because of this workload that was placed on me.

Finally, the great day came. I invited some of my friends from school. Most of the action took place on the bimah, where the leader of the ceremony conducts the crowd. So, there I was, going through the motions, chanting the chant and waiting for this nightmare to be over.

At one point, my hands were clasped behind my back. I felt my father brush my hands away from my tuchus and I heard him mutter, "*Kik nisht git,* it doesn't look good." That sent me into an even higher register.

I continued on and soon there was another whisper, from my uncle or my father, "*Tsu shnel, tsu shnel,* too fast, too fast." I kept thinking, "Am I doing anything right? Is it over yet?"

So, I finished that and then went into my haftarah. I gave my speech and then there was a big lunch afterward. Gifts were all brought forward and the service was *finally* done.

I was so gleeful it was all over. I realized I had made certain mistakes. As I was putting my gifts away, I turned to my father, and I said, "Dad, look at all the gifts I got." And he said something like, "Goddamn you, you son of a bitch." He knocked me down with his words because I didn't perform to my ability.

At that moment, I recognized myself as a failure. Although I was the prized pupil, I finished the day, brought my booty home, and never talked about it again. I was free to follow or not follow the contract with my rabbi. Even though I don't have regrets about not fulfilling my end of the bargain, I always felt guilty about lying to the rabbi. He believed in me, but I let him down.

● ● ● ● ● ● ● ● ●

After Pearl Harbor was attacked on December 7, 1941, my brother Ben joined an Air Force ferrying unit. He was stationed in Texas or Louisiana to receive training. Labe was in junior college at the time. Esther was in Alaska. Eve was in St. Louis.

I remember how excited Labe and I were about the Great War and that America was going to participate. The day we found out, we celebrated in bed regarding America's future glory.

I'm sure we heard whisperings about Hitler and how bad it was for the Jews, but we knew nothing of the full-bloodied story. I suppose we were enthusiastic at the fact that the United States would be pitted against the Jew hater Adolf Hitler. That probably was more reassuring than anything else.

So, 1942 came. I think Labe was flunking out of junior college at the time. He was deeply involved with a non-Jewish girl. I am sure my folks realized he would be drafted soon and were relieved to have that happen. Ben was already with his non-Jewish wife in Texas or Louisiana.

Labe was finally drafted and miracle of miracles was chosen to be part of the Army Specialized Training Program. He would go to school for a short while and learn Japanese. He was taught in Virginia, Moscow, Idaho, and Berkeley, California. He ended up finally being sent to Australia. He would constantly send us letters with updates.

Before he left, I remember Labe saying, "So Ed, think you'll be able to take care of yourself?" implying that my great protector was leaving. However, I never counted on him being there to save me. I was always on my own and able to handle myself. I would miss him but I knew he would be fine.

When the United States reinvaded the Philippines, Labe ended up there. Fortunately, he did not see any action.

Once the war was over, he was sent to Japan and worked out of the building that housed General MacArthur's headquarters. I was not scared for him because he was stationed in areas without much action. Plus, Labe was warped and could talk his way out of any compromising situation.

Another example of Labe's twistedness occurred during his time in Japan. He began collecting cigarettes from as many GIs as he could. He started talking to various store owners and asked whether they would be interested in his American cigarettes. They agreed. So, Labe began selling cigarettes on the black market.

With all his extra loot, Labe was sending money home at the time. We had many relatives who were lieutenants in the military and they wondered how he, a lowly corporal, could be earning all this money, considering they never saw that kind of dough.

After months of selling the cigarettes on the black market, Labe was confronted by an officer who was investigating him. The officer knew what he was doing but spared Labe the indignity of jail time because he was an individual operator and did not belong to a black market gang. The little bastard got off scot-free *again*. Have I mentioned how much I miss him?

After the war, we began to hear all the stories of the Holocaust, which we were not privy to during the war. I think had I known the full severity of the situation, I would have been more concerned for Labe and my people. However, looking back, at that young age, I think it was better that I was kept in the dark.

CHAPTER 3
TO PLAY OR NOT TO PLAY

"Somehow along the way I decided not to fail in my other performances."

In my junior year of high school, I took journalism and radio. I ended up doing a weekly radio show, which was my first tickling of theatrical ambition. By the time I was a senior, I would produce, write, and act in my own radio productions.

At the same time, I concentrated on journalism, particularly because it promised a future. I was also the feature-page editor of the Wyandotte High School *Pantograph*.

I remember one day I was sitting at my desk, thinking about what to put on my feature page and my beloved professor passed by. He asked, "Are you thinking of journalism for a career?" I said, "Yeah," and he replied, "I wouldn't." I asked him why and he said, "You can't make a living." This was in 1947! If you couldn't make a living in journalism back then, when could you?!

My high school consisted of 2,000 kids with roughly seven of them being Jewish. I didn't feel like I fit in so I tried out for football during my freshman year. I didn't make the cut, but each year I persisted and tried out for the team.

I finally made the football team, either the second team or as a reserve, during my junior year. By the time I

My high school picture. I was so fast, I outran my hair.
Courtesy of Asner Family Photo Collection

15

I only bend that far nowadays if I see a dime on the floor.
Courtesy of Asner Family Photo Collection

was a senior, there were only four returning lettermen and they were all in the backfield.

Our coach was a beautiful man and I never honored him enough. His name was Ed Ellis. He had a wonderful attitude, which pushed me to work hard.

We won our first game, which was against Central High School from Kansas City, Missouri. I think our second game was against the powerhouse from the dairy section of Kansas City, Kansas, Shawnee Mission. We beat them: 13–7.

Being undefeated, we built ourselves into a fairly confident team and finally rode into Topeka to play their excellent team. They were strictly a T-formation team. We were a double-wing and single-wing team.

This was our first big trip. When we got there, I tanked up on sweets from the candy store. My sugar rush eventually turned into a sugar crash moments before the big game. A couple of the guys tanked up on beer. As a result, they beat us.

We felt disgraced, but there was nothing we could do about it. The coach wanted to bench one of the guys who was supposedly drinking beer before the game. I had reservations about the punishment because my candy was just as evil as his beer.

One of our last games was against Leavenworth. I saw that it was scheduled on Kol Nidre, the holiest of Jewish holidays. Knowing that I might not be able to play, I immediately told the coach about it. I told my coach that our principal, who was also an enlightened individual, was on the National Conference of the Christians and Jews with my rabbi, and that maybe he could do something.

So, my coach talked to our principal. I guess he talked to the rabbi and, for once, the rabbi redeemed himself. He said, "I can't tell Eddie what to do. He has to leave it to his own conscience."

With enough pressure and guilt hanging over me, the team was busy all week, asking, "You gonna play, you gonna play, you gonna play?"

The day prior to the big game I still hadn't decided what I was going to do. I could hear my mother and brothers downstairs asking my father to allow me to play in the game. He later said to me, "I don't want you to play." And all I could respond was, "Okay, Dad."

So, the big day finally came. I got up and at the bottom of the stairs, my father stood, and before he left for the yard, he said, "Eddie, I don't want you to play. I'm begging you." I said, "Okay, Dad. Okay, okay," and he left for work.

I came down for breakfast, and my mom said, "You're gonna eat your breakfast, go to school, then come home, eat your dinner, and get out of here." Once again, I was the pawn of my brothers and my mother in a conspiracy against my father. But, I listened to her anyway.

I went to Leavenworth. As we were getting dressed for the game, my coach came into the locker room, and he said, "All right guys, I don't want you to go out there and win this for Wyandotte." He said, "I want you to go out there and win this for Eddie!"

So, we went out there and we kicked Leavenworth's ass: 19–7.

Do I regret playing? Well, I ended up being named All-City tackle, and I always questioned whether I deserved the honor.

Our house, on the other hand, was filled with holiday well-wishers and relatives. And the word I received once I got home was, "Okay, everything's okay, you just get up early, and you go to shul (synagogue) with Labe, everything will be alright."

My bones were aching but I got up in the morning and dragged my butt to shul. We sat in the front pew where my father was sitting. He picked up his siddur and tallit, and walked to the back. He refused to sit with us.

The day went on and the women were up on the balcony. Finally, the shofar blew and my brother put out his arms to my father, who gave him a look like, "You son of a bitch." And I, like humble earth, went in and my dad embraced me. I didn't deserve it.

I think that moment was one of the driving forces in my life because I had failed at my bar mitzvah and now I failed at Judaism in the eyes of my father. Somehow along the way I decided not to fail in my other performances.

CHAPTER 4...
GOODBYE COLLEGE, HELLO REAL WORLD

"Thank God actors don't need to be smart."

I worked in radio in high school. I spent years trying to emulate my brother Ben's voice, which had a good rough timber sound to it. However, I didn't think anything about acting at that time. The acting bug didn't hit me until college.

I attended the University of Chicago and during my first year I stayed in the Burton-Judson dormitory. It bordered the Midway and sometime in the winter they decided they were going to start a closed-circuit radio station. My roommate at the time, Jerry Steiner, a chubby little guy from Newark, New Jersey, was involved in the university's drama group called University Theatre.

Jerry considered himself a maven of the theatre. I told him that I did radio in high school. The university's radio group was going to do *Richard II* and I thought that I should read for it. Jerry pompously said, "I don't know, let me hear you read." So, I had a copy of some poetry, I read to him and his mouth fell open. He replied by saying, "Where did you learn to read like that?!"

Weeks later, Jerry came bustling home and said that the drama group was going to do *Murder in the Cathedral* by T. S. Elliot during the summer. He wasn't going to summer school but I was. He said, "Check it out; read it, you can do any of the roles in it!"

So, I did. I did *the* lead, Thomas Beckett. It was my first taste of acting on a real stage. I was officially hooked on acting.

During rehearsals, I found myself being drawn to a woman in the chorus, Joanna. We made googly eyes at each other, and then finally, we went on a date. It was the night before the first matinee. I remember spending my off time reciting the lines of Beckett to her, turning them into lines of passion, and it worked beautifully. I became inspired.

When I started my second year at the University of Chicago, I moved out of the dormitory and took an apartment on 64th and Greenwood. I thought I should bone up on my courses to take the final tests of each course. They told me that even though I had three years of high school Spanish, I could only get out of one quarter. That meant I had to take two more quarters of Spanish. That pissed me off but I studied up on the test, tried to increase my vocabulary as much as I could, and got a B on the final.

I got Cs in the rest of my courses. Physical Science—I think I either flunked or got a D in. Thank God actors don't need to be smart.

I attended the University of Chicago for a full year, summer school, and into Christmas of the following year. When I went home for Christmas vacation, I was down at the junkyard with my brother Labe and my dad. My father sat behind his desk, and he said, "Listen, this letter came for you." And it was a love letter from Joanna. My father asked if she was Jewish. I said, "No."

This was about the time I met Joanna. *Courtesy of Asner Family Photo Collection*

"Well, I want you to stop it," he replied. I told him, "Okay, Dad, okay."

So, Christmas vacation went on and it was finally time to go back to college. In the meantime, Joanna was restless and her folks were going to Europe after New Year's Day. She asked how I would feel if she went with them. I don't recall objecting.

At the time, the University of Chicago was hounding me to be in its next play, which was *Oedipus Rex*. I was to play Creon. Before leaving for Chicago, my dad asked me for a testament that I had broken up with Joanna. I think I said I had or I was going to. At one point, he blew up thinking I wouldn't deliver.

My parents also got a letter from the university saying that I had not been doing much of my coursework. My father told me that he would no longer provide money for school. I knew I either had to push through or drop out. I felt like the biggest loser in the world.

I went back to Chicago feeling totally whipped by the disapproval of my parents. The theatre group kept pressuring me saying, "You gotta stay, you gotta stay, you gotta do Creon." They were using the David Grene translation;

he was a member of the Committee on Social Thought at the university. I finally relented and said, "Okay, I'll do it."

I called home, told my family that I planned to drop out of school, but they wanted me for another play. I told them that I was going to stay and do the play. Joanna went to Europe with her parents and I did *Oedipus Rex*.

David Grene thought I was fantastic. He had been with the Abbey Theatre and he said, "Well, by the time you go, I'll write something for you to serve as an introduction at the Abbey." However, it turned out that the Abbey had instituted new rules that they did not take anybody that didn't know Gaelic.

So, I came home as I was out of funds and laid around the house for a few weeks. I then realized I had to get up and look for a job. First thing I did was join the Encyclopedia Britannica sales group, which was nauseating.

At work, I found the two senior members of the sales group to be the shallow, soulless types. I went into the Fairfax district with the field manager and he made a big deal about the supplements that came with Encyclopedia Britannica. He told me that the supplements could really improve my performance on the job and it would improve my earning capacity.

I learned about hard work in the junkyard.
Courtesy of Asner Family Photo Collection

This guy would find people that didn't have any money and convince them to buy Encyclopedia Britannica. He would see cars on blocks and know that he could convince them to buy these expensive encyclopedias. He was teaching me how to screw people. One time he convinced a woman to sell her children's books to pay for Encyclopedia Britannica. I wanted to piss on the company and the sales force at the same time. I had enough and quit that job.

I got another job selling shoes at a fancy store. We never had a customer. So, that job didn't last long. I continued to look for a job and found out that the Buick and Pontiac plant in Fairfax was hiring. I went down there and they hired me.

I became a spot polisher on the line. It was an open shop and they showed no mercy. It was a swift introduction to the real world.

While working at the plant, I was calling Joanna on the phone all the time. I even rented a post office box so she could write me letters. Before she left for Europe with her parents, I said, "Well, you come down, we'll have a weekend here." However, we were forced to work overtime at the plant on Saturdays.

I decided to call in sick so I could spend the whole weekend with Joanna. I don't know what kind of lie I used for my folks to let them know why I was out of the house, but she came down and we had a great time.

I came to work on Monday and my time card wasn't in the slot. Somebody nearby said, "The general manager wants to see you." So, I go in and there's this older guy sitting in his desk chair.

"You were supposed to work on Saturday," he said.

"Yeah, I know, I was sick."

"Sick? What was wrong with you?" he responded.

"My feet—they hurt me."

"Well, my feet hurt me, too, but I was here," the lazy bastard responded, while sitting in his chair.

He told me that my absence was going as a black mark on my record. I said to myself, "If you only knew how much I didn't care about this job." I had a marvelous time with Joanna and was not going to let the job ruin my high.

The line foreman did not like me. He was red haired, and very nervous, like a wild turkey. He was always on me about the sloppiness of my polishing. Finally, he conned another foreman, who just did hoods and fenders, to take me. That worked out well for a while.

During the course of Joanna's travels in Europe, I used the post office box and got her letters. One day, I got a strange letter from her. It was an exact copy of the one I had already received the week before. She must have xeroxed a copy of the previous letter. I was furious and I knew right there she wasn't thinking of me. Day after day, I envisioned her face on the car hoods and tried to erase it with the aid of a polisher. It didn't work. So, I stopped writing her.

In the meantime, a friend came down from Chicago and wanted me back to do *Julius Caesar*. They wanted me to play Brutus. I was hesitant but he kept urging me and I had nothing happening at home. Except, one day my sister stopped at the drug store where I made all my calls to Joanna. The pharmacist thought this was pretty funny and mentioned something to her. So, she announced it at the dinner table one night. I played dumb. My mom didn't say anything and my dad didn't pursue it. I don't know whether my parents believed it or not, but to me the timing was perfect to go back to Chicago.

Around the same time, I was out with the boys one night and decided I'd give Joanna a call. I called her Chicago number and was told she was at her sister's house in New York. They gave me her number and I called there. However, I didn't reach her; maybe she was sleeping because there was a two-hour time difference.

She eventually called me back and acted full of love. That's when she told me.

"Baby, I'm pregnant."

"What? Whose is it?" I said, knowing it couldn't be mine.

"Yours."

"No, no, no it's not," I responded in complete shock.

The timeline didn't match up. I knew there was no way I could be the father. She simply replied, "Okay." I feebly concluded the call and remember thinking, *What do I tell the boys?* That was the main thing that worried me. To this day, I'm unsure what happened to the baby or if she made the whole thing up. But, I know for a fact, it couldn't have been mine.

Still in shock, I made plans to go back to Chicago and play Brutus. I found a sub-basement apartment where you had to go through a passageway underneath to get to it. I had a fellow roommate, an ex-Marine, who decided to share the apartment with me. It was very nice—concrete floors, throw rugs on them, and everything.

At that time, I desperately needed money. I tried selling television advertising over the phone. I failed at that.

After the play, I finally went to work at the steel mill in Gary, Indiana. I was a hooker helper. It was exciting being around all the steelmaking and all of that, but overall it was boring, very boring.

We were required to work a week on days, then the next week we worked on a swing shift, and the next week we worked on the graveyard shift. The days off alternated, too, so that if you had Saturday and Sunday off in July, you might not see it again until December 25, but that's the way it went.

During this time, I was still on and off again with Joanna. She was hanging around people I wasn't crazy about. Her crowd further alienated her from me.

One of their friends who acquired minor fame as a Jew runner in Palestine asked me if I would mind if he asked her out. I said, "No, no, be my guest." He did and they eventually married. I don't know if I still felt betrayed by her pregnancy, but she was out of my mind at that point anyway.

I ran into her years later while doing a movie in Chicago. She was still married to the same guy. We had lunch and we said goodbye. She was a special part of my college years but the spark was gone—this Kansas hick needed more sophistication and experience.

Even though I never graduated from college, I learned my craft and discovered what eventually would be my passion. I met people who had the same acting ambitions and dreams as me. Without Chicago, I might not be where I am today: *divorced and grouchy.*

CHAPTER 5
THE FRENCH CONNECTION

"At that moment, my life fell into place."

The year was 1949 and even though I vowed to never work in another auto plant, the higher wages at Ford lured me back in. I was hired as a metal finisher. Ford Victorias were the big item on the assembly line at the time. It was also a closed-shop union, which established my pro-union sentiments.

While working at the auto plant, the success of *Oedipus Rex* led the director of the theatre to think he could follow it up with *Antigone*. He was quite eager for me to reprise my role as Creon. The actress who played Antigone was a talented veteran of the USC stage. Her sister was played by Susan Sontag, and Fritz Weaver played Tiresias.

Everything proceeded smoothly with the production until we opened on a Friday night. The next day, David Grene told me that he saw me and liked my performance. He showed up for the matinee on Saturday, and George Blair, the director, called a meeting of the cast afterward.

George turned to the actors of the show and complained about each performance. He went performer to performer and found something nasty to say about each of them. He then looked at me last.

"All because of *him!*" he shouted, while pointing at me.

He said all I did was shout and speculated that I was trying to impress David Grene. He claimed that I had ruined his production, and nobody rose to my defense. I guess in retrospect, they all believed I ruined the show.

I don't know if I was trying to impress David or not, but I did the following two performances and limped through so to speak. I knew I was done, as far as university theatre was concerned.

Thankfully, lo and behold, a new theatre group was being formed with Rene Anselmo, and Paul Sills was a member. Their first production was *Androcles and the Lion*. Mike Nichols was set to play the emperor, Nero. However, the play was too short so they wanted a curtain raiser. They agreed on W. B. Yeats's *Purgatory*. Mike was chosen to direct, and he selected me to play the grandfather of the piece with Jerry Cunliffe playing my grandson.

I was allowed to breathe once again as an actor. *Androcles* and *Purgatory* were successes.

●●●●●●●●●●

I spent a few more weeks in Chicago before coming back to Kansas City to wait for the draft. Floods were covering Kansas City at the time. In early July 1951, I was sent to Camp Crowder in Missouri, but none of the camps were open in the Midwest due to the flooding. So, I was sent to Camp Gordon, now called Fort Gordon, in Georgia for eight weeks of basic training with the Signal Corps.

I hadn't really advertised much that I wanted to be an actor. There was a time when I was in Monmouth, New Jersey, where I went into the Special Services office and introduced myself. I said, "I just wanted you to know that I'm an actor and I wanted to see if you would place me in Special Services." The officer said, "We're fifty miles from New York City, what the hell do we want you for?"

There went that dream. So, I moved on to start my civic duty as a radarman.

When I first started in the Signal Corps, we would be in a classroom for a week and learn the basics of radar sets. We would then put our knowledge to work and monkey with the sets for a week or so. We'd then come back to the classroom and take a test on what we learned.

I remember one particular test. At that point, our class had too many people, so they divided us into two sections. The first group took the test, while the second group waited.

I was in the second group and would always hear the first group come out and say, "The G2s are no good." That's not what we wanted to hear. We all knew that if we flunked enough tests, we would be shipped to Korea. *None* of us wanted that.

So, my turn came. I started taking the test, and when I could, I looked over my shoulder to see what answers the other guys were putting. The guy in front of me had a high-scoring G2 and the two guys on the side of me were skilled electricians.

Don't get me wrong, we all cheated on the test, but I was the only one in the class that got one hundred percent. They all knew I cheated so everyone in class started saying, "Let Asner give the critique!" What a bunch of ingrates!

I was eventually sent overseas to a 150-man post. I ended up in a placement camp in Germany for about a week or so, and then I was shipped to South Central France for about ten months. I was stationed in the town of Saumur, just north of Poitiers.

First, I was placed in a training section, but they didn't really have a need for me there. They didn't know what to do with me so they put me in the orderly room. I was with a training officer named Hurt.

While working with him, I could tell that the training was just a lot of gibberish. So, I decided to revise the two-page training schedule for the post. Since much of the information was repetitive, I used a lot of ditto marks. By the time I finished revising it, the schedule was less than a page.

Hurt looked at the schedule one day.

"Ehhhh, I'm not sure that I like the way that schedule looks. It looks too short to me," he said.

"Well, they're ditto marks."

"Yeah, well, I'd rather you type it out," he responded.

"Okay, I'll type it out."

That was my duty. Pretty exciting, eh?

Eventually, my post decided to start a basketball team. I played for the sheer pleasure of working out. Of the men who showed up, there was a tall Kentuckian that the captain felt would be a good leader. As it turned out, he had zero character. He was totally lacking in leadership and drive.

One day while I was in the orderly room with the captain, I complained about his inability to lead. My captain said, "Fine, you lead." Since we were getting invitations to play French teams at this time, I said, "Okay if I get Joe Brook," who spoke French. So, I was put in charge of the basketball team.

Our first invitation was to play the team from Angers, France. The game displayed to me how out of shape our players were. All the French team did was play defense and sling the ball to their man under the basket. That's how they beat us.

With each game, we got better and better. The men were conditioned and our fundamentals of basketball improved. The French could no longer afford to keep a man under the basket because our team was too good. We started winning and my team became a force to be reckoned with.

I eventually took leave in Spain and was sent home shortly after, but I heard later that my team was regarded as the second best in Europe. They played in a tournament against the French national team and lost by one point because the officiating was rigged.

Even though my time in the military was uneventful, I guess the best service I did for my country was to keep the team going. I helped shape the team so our country was well-represented and not an embarrassment.

Just before I left France in 1953, I got a letter from Paul Sills, who I knew at the university. He said, "You better come join us, we're gonna start a theatre group in Chicago. We're going to do old plays, old classics, and new plays." The theatre was called Playwrights Theatre Club.

At that moment, my life fell into place.

One depressed Jew (*Rich but Happy*).
Courtesy of the Estate of Paul Sills

CHAPTER 6...
A BUNCH OF COMMIES

"She was lovely...she let me eat half of her steak."

Playwrights Theatre Club, later known as the Compass Players, was the start of my acting career. Playwrights was founded by Paul Sills, Eugene Troobnick, and David Shepherd. The group included Barbara Harris, along with Mike Nichols and Elaine May, only in a more limited sense.

At the time Paul contacted me, he was acting and directing. Later, we both performed in *The Tempest* together. I played Prospero and he was the King. I respected him enormously and he respected me.

Paul's mother, Viola Spolin, was a well-known acting teacher. Some of that awe was bestowed upon him because of her. She wrote this book entitled *Theater Games*, which is still highly regarded. To me though, Paul was far more brilliant.

I arrived in Chicago on the opening night of *Round Dance*. The audience responded well and seemed to love the production. I knew this was something special and was excited to start performing with the group.

When we first started, we were so-called amateurs. During those first months, we were a group of raggle-taggle gypsies. Everyone in the group was enthusiastic about what we were doing, and that became more evident in each performance.

The following Monday we started production on Büchner's *Wozzeck*, from which the opera of the same name was taken. *Wozzeck* established me as a principal

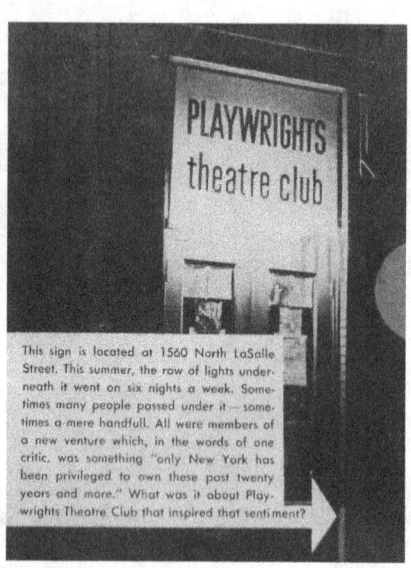

This sign is located at 1560 North LaSalle Street. This summer, the row of lights underneath it went on six nights a week. Sometimes many people passed under it — sometimes a mere handfull. All were members of a new venture which, in the words of one critic, was something "only New York has been privileged to own these past twenty years and more." What was it about Playwrights Theatre Club that inspired that sentiment?

There is where it all started.
Courtesy of the Estate of Paul Sills

A Jew playing a Jew.
Courtesy of the Estate of Paul Sills

performer of the group. The feeling on the stage was exhilarating. It was like nothing I had felt before as an actor. I couldn't wait for my other performances.

During the early 1950s, Playwrights Theatre Club was spat on by some in Chicago for being a "bunch of commies." This all started when, on our off night, which was Monday, we decided to rent the theatre to whomever wanted to rent it.

Studs Terkel, who evidently was connected to several communist groups, was doing a roundup of various folk singers and national singers. After advertising the show as being in our theatre, we got one reply back with a very nicely developed stamp.

The theatre is my roots.
Courtesy of the Estate of Paul Sills

"Fight CommUNism," the stamp read.

Also, on it, the person wrote in red pencil or red grease, "Keep this red out of Chicago," and had Terkel's name circled. Unintimidated, we put the show on anyway and it went very well.

We were constantly aware of sociopolitical sensitivities. For example, when the theatre opened, the opening show was *The Caucasian Chalk Circle*. Critic Claudia Cassidy came and wrote a review, and I don't even know if it was good or bad, but she ended it by writing, "Unfortunately, Playwrights and I walk on different sides of the political street." And she never came back. She was the big reviewer at the time in Chicago. She's the critic that saved *The Glass Menagerie*. So, you win some, you lose some.

Herman Kogan of the *Chicago Sun-Times* adored us, as did Sydney Harris of the *Chicago Daily News*. They always gave us good reviews. Roger Dettmer of the *Chicago American* always found some way of slamming us. But, we found a way to go on.

There came a time when the so-called "commies" of Hollywood made a film called *Salt of the Earth* about striking miners in Arizona. It was labeled as a "commie" film because it was not studio financed or approved. The movie didn't go anywhere and was only exhibited through showings.

Paul and David okayed a screening of the film without any of us knowing. They were aware that we were fighting the communist tar every day and that we might disapprove of their decision.

Fellow actors in the group, Zohra Lampert and Bill Alton, her husband, brought up the question to the other actors: Should they go ahead and okay something like this, when we are walking the line so carefully? We discussed it and agreed that the actors should have the right to voice their opinions.

So, we voted against the film screening. I voted against it because I believed it was too dangerous. I felt guilty but those were the kind of steps I was taking at the time because I

Here I am out of makeup.
Courtesy of the Estate of Paul Sills

cared more about furthering my career. Paul and David swallowed their pride and put up money so the film could be screened at another theatre.

Eventually, Playwrights ended in 1955, and our last production was at a rented hall downtown with William Marshall as Oedipus and I was the leader of the chorus.

In the meantime, Paul was busy developing the Compass Players, the predecessor to the Second City. Mike Nichols and Elaine May, who were doing small stuff with us in Playwrights, got together and began doing improvisation as part of the Compass Players. The other actors, other than Zohra, were all eager to be a part of it. So, they started performing at a bar down on the South Side.

I, on the other hand, wanted to take my good reviews and capitalize on them. I expected to go to New York City. And I did.

• • • • • • • • •

There I was in the City That Never Sleeps, New York. I lived in a railroad flat filled with cockroaches and bedbugs. The civil rights movement was in full force, but I was not looking to get involved in any political movement.

I owe so much to Paul Sills and my fellow actors.
Courtesy of the Estate of Paul Sills

I dedicated myself to making the rounds in New York City to every agent's and producer's office I could find. It became almost like a clockwork routine.

So, I walked the streets and I laid the city out like a grid. I took the latest *Variety* and checked all the addresses. I would mark the city, piece by piece. I went to agents' offices, dropped off headshots, and made nice with the secretaries. I'm sure they threw the pictures in the wastebaskets as soon as I left. I never expected to get anything out of it, but things started happening.

I went and saw Carmen Capalbo and Stanley Chase at the Theatre de Lys. We had previously done a pirated version of *The Threepenny Opera* in Chicago. We didn't pay any royalties or anything and, of course, would've been sued if we had any money. I asked them for a role in one of their productions, but they had no openings at that time.

In December 1955, I was slated to do a role in an off-night production of *Venice Preserved* at the Phoenix Theatre. I don't think I even had lines. My main job was to howl like a wolf, which was the cue for the conspirators in the play to assemble.

During that time, Carmen called me to take over a role in *Threepenny*. I wanted to kick myself because I had already committed to *Venice*. Carmen said, "Don't worry, there will be other openings."

So, I did the showcase and it was kind of laughable. Two months later, after my commitment to *Venice* was over, I got another call from Carmen to take over the role of Bob the Saw, one of the gang members in *Threepenny*. I jumped at the opportunity.

Jerry Orbach, Jerry Stiller, and John Astin were in it at the time. Scott Merrill played Macheath and Jo Wilder was the starlet. In addition to playing Bob the Saw, I was the understudy for Tiger Brown, Commissioner of Police.

We were going along quite nicely, and Frank Perry, who was a director, was one of the gang. Maury Shrog, Joe Elic, and Bea Arthur were also parts of the production. It opened in early 1956.

I felt very lucky to find myself engaged in a 300-seat theatre in New York City. The cast was great and, week after week, people came to see the show. I felt successful.

During my time in the play, I remember feeling agitated every time I gave a speech to the audience. For some reason, John Astin and Stefan Gierasch would make a lot of noise upstage of me.

Evidently, Fred Downs, who played Peachum in a prior appearance, was also upset at their disruptions. At one point, he finally had enough and threw a fish at them during his performance.

They were good guys though. Jerry Orbach, John Astin, Jerry Stiller, and I would always play cards in a room above the stage before our cues. Many times, we would run down the stairs barely making our entrances on time. I'm sure the audience wondered what that thunderous noise was before each of us took the stage.

I performed throughout the year, and during that time, Jerry Orbach and I would always go out for Sunday dinners between shows, and we generally would eat at Verney's, which was just up the street. The owner, Richard Verney, also played Tiger Brown in the show.

One night, Frank Perry went with us to get steaks, and he said, "You guys want steak? Next week we'll go to my girlfriend's place, and I'll fix you guys some steaks." Jerry and I said, "Great."

Next weekend came, we showed up at his girlfriend's apartment, and she had brought her friend, Nancy. She immediately caught my eye. She was lovely. Plus, she let me eat half of her steak. She had me from that moment on.

Nancy announced that she was going in for minor surgery the next day. So, I found out what hospital and room she was in and took her some flowers. I like to think I won her over at that moment.

Jerry and I were very close friends when we were both getting started. I miss him.
Courtesy of Chris Orbach

At that time, Nancy was going with some power player in theatre, whose name was also Eddie. My girlfriend had left town to be at The Premise, an improv in St. Louis. Her name was also Nancy. We could talk in our sleep all we wanted and nobody would get indicted.

So, I asked her out on a date.

It became a tradition for Nancy and me to go to 42nd Street on Saturday nights. We'd catch a double feature there and then we'd go get something to eat. Dawn would break and then we'd get something for breakfast. It was beautiful. And, so was she.

During this whirlwind romance, I had to go through the grind of doing eight shows a week. I did that for a couple years. I remember that Jerry Orbach started going with a village character named Marta, who befriended Nancy and me. We became a foursome.

We also had another friend who played poker with us. His name was Ben Hayes, and his wife was Irene. So, we'd all get together and we'd go to 42nd Street on Saturday night and see double features. Then eventually a fourth guy materialized, who was a fascinating fellow, named Bob Darnell.

Bob had an interesting past. He was in the Marines and eventually became a member of Mickey Cohen's gang. Someone ultimately snitched on him and he was sent to San Quentin. His chest was covered with knife marks. Evidently, he survived an attack in jail and said he didn't remember anything that had happened during the fight until two or three months later.

So, the group all got together on Saturday nights, Jerry, Marta, Ben, Irene, Bob, Nancy, and me. Nancy slowly became more and more a part of my life and eventually moved in with me.

After she moved in, I adopted a six-toed cat named Biriki, which I am told means "one-two" in Turkish. I'll let my faithful readers challenge me if I am wrong.

Not too long after, Nancy decided that she wanted a cat for herself as well. She heard that a kitten was in need of adoption in Brooklyn. It was a bobbed-tail Siamese. Biriki got into a fit at first sight of the kitten, but they eventually teamed up and became fond of each other.

So, there we were, living together and adopting cats. What could be more romantic?

We realized early on that marriage was in our future, and we likely would have been married years earlier if it hadn't been for my parents. You see, Nancy was an Episcopalian. I was afraid to tell my Orthodox parents because they discouraged my siblings from intermarriage in the past.

After my father died, we told my mother of our intent to marry. She responded as I expected. She insisted that Nancy convert to Judaism. And, God bless Nancy, she agreed. Thankfully, we found a progressive rabbi who allowed us to marry with a *mild* conversion. I like to call it "Jewish Lite."

Nancy and I married on March 23, 1959, my mom's birthday, in a civil ceremony at the Park Sheraton Hotel in New York City. Nancy's parents planned the entire event. The only family member of mine who could attend was my sister Eve. Many of our friends were present including Jerry and Marta Orbach, Ben and Irene Hayes, Stanley and Deborah Schneider, and Noam and Jessie Pitlik.

Bob Smith, who was in our theatre group in Chicago, was my best man. He was the sweetest guy in the world so I wanted to honor him by having him stand with me during the ceremony.

My bride, a regular sex pistol.
Courtesy of Asner Family Photo Collection

Our wedding was small, but wonderful. We were surrounded by friends and family. I still can't believe that such a beautiful woman thought that I was worthy of being her husband. I must have done something right in a past life to deserve her.

Life was finally coming together. I had a beautiful wife, a good agent, and was in New York City working as a professional actor. My hard work in Chicago finally paid off. However, there was a feeling that something was missing. I was still awaiting that *big* break in my career.

CHAPTER 7

PURSUING THE TRUTH

"I'm a better actor, and person, because of them."

I went through a phase with *The Threepenny Opera* where I so hated what I was doing that I put myself through hell. No matter what kind of preparation I went through, I feared I was going to black out while performing a scene. I spent two or three nights fighting that blackout and under the mortal terror that I was going to lose it at any second.

It was not until I reached the brink of actual blacking out that I felt I passed the test. I moved on to the second scene, then the third, and then the fourth. I was living through the worst inflicted hell I could ever imagine. My body was telling me, "Get out…get out…get out. You are not behaving like a learning actor." I burned out.

Thankfully, at the time the two producers of *Ivanov* wanted me to take over the role of Borkin. Jack Bittner was starring in it. The play was being performed in a small theatre and had a wonderful cast. I'd be getting less money, but I'd be free. So, I took the part and felt free. And, boy, I did a hell of a job. I was back to learning to be an actor.

At this time, I was studying with Mira Rostova, who was a great teacher. She had been the mentor for Montgomery Clift,

Theatre was my training ground for all the work I did in TV and film.
Courtesy of Asner Family Photo Collection

and later Jessica Lange. I had previously worked with Stella Adler for a short time, but I didn't care for her. Mira was a breath of fresh air. With her, I even had an opportunity to take scene studies with Lee Strasberg.

Strasberg was an interesting character. I remember a scene with this girl named Audrey. She was a writer and she was doing this three-person scene with a guy, who acted as Jane Fonda's guru at the time, Andreas Voutsinas.

So, the scene goes on and at the end she's with Andreas. He pulls her to him and he kisses her. After the scene ended, Audrey burst into tears and said, "He bit me!"

Immediately after, Andreas stomped his foot on the ground and said, "She changed the blocking!" In theatre, blocking is typically where an actor is supposed to stand on the stage, for dramatic effect, lighting, and audience viewpoints. Lee then tried to act as the judge to determine who was at fault.

Both sides were equally condemned. I thought to myself, *Lee is not for me. He's going to condemn him equally for biting her, no more than he's going to condemn her for changing the blocking? What kind of bullshit is that?!*

I also recall seeing Lee display favoritism toward pretty young girls. I thought, *If he's not fair and balanced with them, then that's another black mark.*

I performed one scene for the class, and he didn't have anything to say. I guess it was a good thing, but I felt like I wasn't acting. I was executing, not acting.

There was implied criticism from Lee, but there was nothing to comment on so I performed it as it should be performed. There was nothing emotionally in the scene. So, he really couldn't put his hooks into me.

Even though I adored Mira, working with Lee Strasberg was political for me. He was a powerhouse in New York City at the time, and I wanted the stature of being at the Actors Studio.

I had done a couple of scenes for other actors trying out for the Actors Studio, but they never amounted to anything. They didn't understand me. So, I was never invited to join. Over time, I really lost interest in joining. I have a feeling that I probably would not have adjusted well to the method taught by the studio.

Mira's system worked for me. To be honest, I think I did her system unconsciously. So, there was little to bend or sway me. Her system was a structure of supporting every one of your choices.

There was one time I did a scene, which got criticized. I performed Iago to Malachi Throne's Othello. I chose to do it as a real guy from the streets, rough and ready, almost overlaying the evil drive that drove him. It didn't work. I wanted to show him as the rough military man, as opposed to the evil incarnate.

I could tell by the reaction of my fellow classmates that my interpretation was failing from the beginning. I knew no matter how sincere my objective was that I failed to embody it properly. I was so busy making him a man of the streets that I blanketed the evil intent inherent in his lines. You can pursue one truth, but if you do so by masking the truth in the lines, then you fail.

Mira taught me to trust my own instincts. I think she knew it too. My most successful scene with Mira was probably my audition scene with her, which I performed with Zohra Lampert. We did *For Esmé—with Love and Squalor.* I was calm and relaxed, almost nonexistent, which was required by the narrator of *For Esmé.*

Years later, I ran into Mira and told her that her method always worked for me. She then proudly told me that she changed her teaching technique. I couldn't believe it! I found nothing wrong with her method or teaching style. When it ain't broke, don't fix it!

Director Sidney Lumet reminded me of Mira in some aspects. We worked on the movie *Daniel* together. The movie was based on Julius and Ethel Rosenberg, who were convicted and executed by the United States for being spies for the Soviet Union. I played the couple's lawyer.

In the film, the children are left with their grandmother, who was not properly supporting them or taking care of them. So, I have a talk with her. I became almost steel-jawed in the scene, yelling, "Wake up woman! Get with it! Do your job!" Then Lumet said, "No, let's try it totally stressless, almost no energy. No volume, no sharpness." My performance almost became a whisper in the scene. I said, "These are your grandchildren," almost whispering in her ear. That was the take that they used.

Another example of this was director Leo Penn. I was doing the television drama *Slattery's People,* and I had asked out of my contract. They said they'd let me out of my contract as long as I'd come back and do whatever shows they had written for me. I agreed.

So, when I returned, Leo was brought in to direct the episode. The script dealt with privileged information where I refused to divulge my sources and was eventually put in jail. Richard Crenna was the star, and I starred in two scenes with him, among others.

In the first scene, I was drunk and high, which is how I performed it. When it came time for the second scene, my character was still drinking so I started to do the scene in the same way that I did the first one. Leo said, "No, no, no, no. We did that. We're going to do it a different way. It has to be a different choice. You can't just be drunk again; you have to do something different." Right there, I learned never to repeat myself as an actor.

Similarly, somewhere along the way I did a Rod Serling script. It was a ninety-minute movie. I played an airport manager and Jack Lord was the FBI man; he worked constantly with me on those scenes. At one point, I thought, *Oh man, I'm so smooth; I'm making this schmuck look like chopped liver.* Then I saw the clip and each scene was a carbon copy of the previous scene.

I was pursuing the truth and doing it differently is an imposition. Every writer writes a script as the truth, and there's only one way to do the truth. Sidney Lumet and Leo Penn showed me different ways to perform and drew it from me. Sydney Pollack also had a sense, a feeling for each scene. He had an understanding of what to do before I realized what to do. His direction was always good.

Most directors are delivery boys, but the best directors are teachers, and the best teachers are directors. Both need to visualize the best approach to a scene and how to draw the best performance from an actor.

Even during my cockiest moments, I remember Mira and these directors because they taught me that there is always room for improvement. Every actor should consider themselves a student for life. There is always a way to perfect your character and bring something new to a performance. I'm a better actor, and person, because of them.

● ● ● ● ● ● ● ● ● ● ●

I was slowly working my way up on television. I had a role on *Studio One*. I'd also been doing Sunday morning shows and did well there. I performed on *Camera Three, Look Up and Live,* and *Lamp Unto My Feet.*

I did a couple episodes of *Naked City* in Los Angeles in 1961. I played Lieutenant Vincent Busti. The first time I appeared on the show, I got shot. Robert Duvall played the head of the gang that shot me.

The second time, they got Paul Burke and me. We were sent to Los Angeles to extradite two brothers, Bobby Blake and Frank Sutton. Blake later became known for his role on *Baretta,* and Sutton played the tough drill sergeant on *Gomer Pyle, U.S.M.C.*

So, we're there to extradite these two guys and we go to the courthouse to participate in the extradition hearing. While we were at the hearing, Sutton's character grabbed a gun out of the deputy's holster and shot his way out of the courtroom. Once again, I got shot.

In the meantime, Paul Burke goes on in the episode and participates in the chase. He eventually recaptures one of the two brothers.

So, those were the two Lieutenant Bustis that I played on *Naked City*. The producers must have heard I came from New York City because they sure loved killing me.

Working on that show was a big break for me. While I was in Los Angeles, I remember calling Nancy.

"I think I want to stay another week to map out the lay of the land here."

"Oh, shit," she eloquently responded.

So, after a week spent mapping out Los Angeles, I called her again.

"I got a guy who wants to represent me. I think I'd like to move out."

"Oh, shit," she responded.

My wife sure had a way with words. Despite the crippling enthusiasm she displayed during the phone calls, Nancy quickly got ready for the move. My mother and brother Ben chipped in and bought us a Chevy Impala. Nancy arranged for a U-Haul that we could pull, hired professional packers, and sublet our apartment.

We arrived in California during Memorial Day weekend. Our first home in Los Angeles was an apartment above a garage at the crossroads of Woodrow Wilson Drive and Mulholland Drive, right next to the Belgian consulate.

So, the hunt began. I was officially a Hollywood actor. Now, if only my agent, Jack Fields, could get me any jobs.

CHAPTER 8···
HOLLYWOOD HUSTLE

"How ridiculous that was, trying to hit James Arness."

After years of learning my craft as an actor in Chicago and New York City, I continued to get bit parts in films and guest appearances on television shows throughout the 1960s. Even though my big role didn't come till years later, I began making an actual living as an actor in Hollywood.

I appeared on an episode of *Route 66* on our way to California. We stopped in Youngstown, Ohio. It was the first of five episodes I appeared on. Every time, I went to a different city. It was exciting because I was acting, but also exploring the country. Other than Youngstown, we filmed in Cleveland, Ohio, as well as the states of Louisiana and Arizona.

After the move, I went to the unemployment office so I could earn some money between projects. There were two *long* lines of people waiting to get in. Of course, they decided to merge the lines into one.

So, everyone was scuffling, trying to get ahead of the people in the other line. This little guy jumped in front me.

I was fuming. My angry stare was practically burning a hole in the back of his sports coat. He could tell I was mad, too, because he kept taking little looks back at me, flashing a smile. I think he was trying to apologize and diffuse the awkward situation, but I was having none of that. Then it hit me.

It was Harpo Marx.

I was certainly starstruck. I mean, this was my first week in Hollywood and there is this comedy legend right in front of me. Did I talk to him? Hell no, the little bastard stole my spot in line! No one gets a pass after cutting in front of me.

I was then featured on several episodes of *The Play of the Week* television series. One episode was actually written by Rod Serling. Ralph Nelson was the big Hollywood director brought in to direct the episode. The premise centered on desegregation in a small southern town. It was such an important script with a powerful message. However, I remember feeling disappointed with the way Nelson directed it. He could have done so much more with the script Serling gave him. The end result felt pretty mediocre.

Working on *Outlaws* was another big break for me. I got to meet Slim Pickens. I loved Slim. One day we were talking and he was saying how when he filmed the movie *One-Eyed Jacks*, director Marlon Brando (yes, *director* Marlon Brando) said, "I want your characters to get in a fight over here." So, actor Tim Carey responded, "Yeah, yeah, I gotta do this to Slim and I gotta do that to Slim."

Brando yelled, "Action!" and Carey started connecting with Slim, actually hitting him. Slim was practically puking from the beating he was taking. So, he thought, "Okay, now I can hit him, it's on!" And, of course, Slim was a well-built man and in great shape. Heck, he had been a rodeo clown for years!

So, in the next take, Brando yelled, "Action!" and Slim kicked the shit out of Carey. That was Slim, one tough son of a bitch.

Then came *Alfred Hitchcock Presents*. I played Warden Bragan. R. G. Armstrong was a guest star. Hitchcock wasn't there for the taping, but it was certainly a thrill to have my name attached to Hitchcock, regardless of how minor a connection it was.

During this time, I also worked on a movie called *Kid Galahad* with Elvis Presley. I played Assistant District Attorney Frank Gerson. I had one scene with Elvis, but he was only in the background. I primarily dealt with actor Gig Young.

At that time, Elvis always had an entourage around him. He was also busy breaking boards with his hands between takes. He did extreme stuff like that, but he was a good guy and nice to be around.

I think Elvis was trying to do too much, especially breaking boards. I think he actually had a broken hand during filming. But, that's the kind of guy he was. He was adventurous but never caused a disruption on set.

Sometime later, I did a second movie with Elvis. It was called *Change of Habit,* and Mary Tyler Moore was in it. Even though Mary was in the movie, I didn't have a scene with her.

At this point, Elvis's style had changed. He was no longer breaking boards and there was no entourage around him anymore, but he was slick. You could see that all the women were quite happy to be in his company. He certainly was a charmer.

The early 1960s were an especially busy time for me as an actor. I had already worked with Elvis and on big shows like *Outlaws* and *Alfred Hitchcock Presents* so my résumé was certainly developing. That led to roles on *The*

Lieutenant, *The Virginian*, *Dr. Kildare*, and *Ben Casey*. I was making a name for myself as a character actor.

Stoney Burke was a lot of fun because I remember watching the show at home and noticing Jack Lord's character get hurt in a scene.

In the episode, they cut to a doctor's office and you see his character being bandaged up. However, you could tell that they weren't using Jack Lord's back in the shot. I couldn't wait to get on the show just to find out whose back was being used.

So, I finally got a role on *Stoney Burke* with Warren Oates as the costar. I was very excited to meet him.

"You gotta tell me, you gotta tell me," I said.

"What?" he asked.

"You had this episode a month ago and Jack Lord got hurt."

"That wasn't his back was it?"

"No, no, that wasn't his back," Warren said.

He told me that Lord actually had a casting call to find an actor to play his back! That's Hollywood for ya! Now, if only I could cast an actor to play my hairline…

After *Stoney Burke*, I appeared on *The Alfred Hitchcock Hour*, my second brush with Hitchcock. I played the father of this kid who was a psychopath. He set fires and tried to kill our neighbors. My character refused to believe suspicions about his son. It had an all-star cast including Bradford Dillman and Diana Hyland. It was very well done.

From there I went on to *The Eleventh Hour* with Wendell Corey. I remember at the time I was going to do an episode of *The Untouchables,* which was a potential backdoor pilot for a series. It would star Barbara Stanwyck with me costarring.

The series never got off the ground, but when Wendell found out that I'd be working with Barbara Stanwyck he said, "You gotta—you gotta wait." So, he ran and got an old 8 × 10 of his, and autographed it.

"When we worked together, Barbara was such a fucking stickler, that if we didn't begin right on the minute that the call was, then it bugged her," he said.

"She drove me nuts with it, so, when I did show up on time, I waited outside the stage door for five or ten minutes just to piss her off all the more!"

I did eventually give Barbara the autographed photo, and she responded like Wendell described her—she scoffed at me and blew it off. Perhaps I was lucky that pilot was not picked up.

That same year, I was cast on *The Outer Limits*. I loved the show so I was delighted to get hired on it. Barbara Luna and Steve Marlowe costarred with me. The only problem was that the monster in it had to be imagined by me, which was difficult. I pretended to be scared of something that I couldn't see while filming.

I was hoping that the finished product would be better than the filming experience. Unfortunately, I didn't care for the completed episode because it didn't have the phenomenal mystique that the earlier episodes had. I guess they can't all be home runs.

I was also a big fan of *Gunsmoke* when I got a role on the show. I loved and admired James Arness. I always felt my appearance was absurd because in one particular episode, I played a drunken army sergeant, who spent the weekend in jail. And, finally, when James lets me go, I take a swing at him.

I thought how ridiculous that was, trying to hit James Arness. He was a beast of a man!

All my guest roles were paying off because I was easily able to transition from television to film. I had the opportunity in 1965 to work with Anne Bancroft, Sidney Poitier, and Telly Savalas in *The Slender Thread*. I played Detective Judd Ridley. Bancroft's character was suicidal and I was the detective in charge of finding her. The role was a significant upgrade over my previous movie roles. I had more lines and got to work with director Sydney Pollack, who I adored.

Like the movie says, "Must Love Dogs."
Courtesy of Asner Family Photo Collection

● ● ● ● ● ● ● ● ● ●

Even with my busy schedule, I actually had a fairly normal home life. Though we had disagreements, Nancy was the ideal wife. When we got our first apartment in Los Angeles, I was busy watching *The Honeymooners* while Nancy was making her typical great dinners.

We both had a love for nature and spent much of our time in California relishing in the wildlife that surrounded us. One day, we heard a rustling in the avocado tree just outside our apartment. We pulled back our curtains and there hanging in the tree were two raccoons, lying on their backs and eating avocados. We both looked at each other and knew that we were home.

All this time, I was delighted to be working like I had never worked before. I was also making money like I had never earned before. It felt great knowing that Nancy could have anything she desired at the time.

My twins were born in September 1963. Nancy only gained eleven pounds during her pregnancy. Did I mention she was pregnant with *twins?!* I think they weighed a combined ten pounds, so all in all Nancy only gained a pound! Unbelievable!

We had a son and a daughter. My son was born first. Nine minutes later came my daughter. I was so relieved we had a daughter because I didn't think I could handle raising two boys at the same time. My daughter stayed in the hospital for an additional week because she was severely underweight when she was born.

I remember when I brought her home from the hospital, we were having a heat wave in Los Angeles and there was no air conditioning in my car.

We've been divorced a long time, but I still love her.
Courtesy of Asner Family Photo Collection

When I finally got to the house, her little round face looked like a boiled potato. She was certainly a trooper!

The twin situation worked out well because my mother had been badgering us to name a child after her. But we didn't know the sex of the children before they were born. So, when our daughter came, this was my mom's opportunity to really pressure us.

However, it was a Jewish tradition to name your children after a deceased family member. My aunts were very troubled that we were thinking of breaking this code by naming our daughter after my living mother.

Nancy and I consulted with a rabbi, and we were told that it was a *custom* to name your child after a deceased relative, not a *law*. So, we were free to name our children whatever we wanted.

My greatest achievement is my children.
Courtesy of Asner Family Photo Collection

We named our son Matthew, after my father, Morris. Well, starting with an *M* was sufficient. That counts, right? And, we named our daughter Liza, after my mother, Lizzie. That sure made my mother happy.

Nancy was a good mother. I can certainly say that both kids adored her. One issue, however, I can remember with the twins was that everyone was so charmed by how cute Liza was, which meant Matt was neglected. I guess I was guilty of giving Liza more attention as well. Nancy became fiercely protective of Matt because of that. She didn't want him to feel left out. I think that created a divide and so-called rivalry between us.

The twins were followed in 1967 by my daughter Katie. She was going to be named Susan until I marched into the hospital room and told Nancy that I preferred Katherine. Thus, it was to be.

Katie was a beautiful child and spoiled by everyone, to such an extent that, when she was old enough to share with the twins, she began to resent that she wasn't a twin herself. Whenever sharing took place between Liza and Matt, she insisted that she receive her fair share as well. If they had an ice cream bar, she had to have an ice cream bar. If they got jacks, she got jacks.

Liza was very easygoing. She would cave to Katie all the time. It drove me nuts! I wanted her to stand up for herself more. Matt, on the other hand, was always happy to take his share.

I never had a problem juggling my home life, work, and the kids. When work took me away from home, if at all feasible, my family came with me. It was our way of exploring America and taking trips together.

Life was good, but I took Nancy for granted. She cared for the kids, cleaned the apartment, cooked dinner, and was always there for me. By doing all of this, I was able to pursue acting. I wouldn't be where I am today without her sacrifices.

• • • • • • • • •

When I got a role in *El Dorado* with John Wayne, I thought the role was relatively small. However, when I showed up at Paramount Studios, I told actor Jim Davis that I had been hired for a week to work in Tucson, Arizona.

"No, no, no," he said. "Once director Howard Hawks gets you down there, he will keep you there."

I called my agent and told him that they'd have to safeguard me because I would not be coming back to Los Angeles in a week, as originally expected. Luckily, he got me a larger contract and I went to Tucson.

I was in the first scene that was shot. In the scene, Wayne pulls up on his horse and tells me that he will not assassinate the sheriff I paid him to kill. The sheriff, who was played by Robert Mitchum, was supposedly a friend of Wayne's character.

After we shot the scene, I made some suggestions to Hawks. He seemed to approve and wanted to try them out. Of course, that delayed the filming. I am sure Wayne was delighted.

Hawks then said, "It's going to take a good while to set up the shot," and told me to go back to my trailer. I started wandering around and saw Wayne working with his Appaloosa, doing tricks.

As I got closer, I heard, "Where's that New York actor?" At the time, I had already been in California for a couple years so I said, "You mean me?" He mumbled something at me that I couldn't make out. So, I moved on. I realized by "New York actor" he meant "Jew." He probably had already written me off as an extreme liberal.

I then went back to the set to rehearse the scene. In the scene, Wayne's character had to throw a bag of money at me. During one rehearsal, he threw the bag and I dropped it. I really felt like the "New York Jew" at that point.

I then rehearsed the scene again. This time when the scene was finished, I threw the money toward him and it fell to the ground. He missed it.

The next time, he threw the money at me without looking and I caught it by instinct. He then made a comment about the Dodgers being in the World Series and that I should get out there with a glove and show them how to catch.

So, we shot Wayne's scenes, and it was finally time to reverse camera and film me. Before we started, Hawks looked uneasy and then took me behind the set.

"Something is not working—" he said.

"I know what it is," I interrupted. "I am in awe working with John Wayne and having difficulty thinking my character can buy and sell his character. I need to remind myself of this while I do the scene."

I told myself that John Wayne didn't exist. I did the scene with that mindset, and it was evidently perfect for Hawks. He then used me as an example to the younger actors. I was flattered.

Nancy and the twins came down to Old Tucson while I was filming. We all explored together. This was our first big adventure. We hadn't really traveled as a family up until that point. It was wonderful being able to show them their old man at work.

Another memory I have of working on the set was that I had a large suite at the motel, which lay between Hawks's suite and Wayne's suite. After Nancy and the kids went home, I'd get together with the stuntmen and actors in my room. Robert Mitchum even joined us once.

One night, my suite got pretty loud so we adjourned to a stuntman's room. We played poker there, still making noise. I then went to bed. I was off work the next day, but I was awakened by the assistant director very early in the morning.

He reported to me that Hawks was very angry. Hawks then came by and said that everyone had to be in Old Tucson each night, and if I didn't like it, I could "go back to Los Angeles."

I was officially on his shit list.

After a few nights had past, I told Larry Butterworth, who was the makeup man for John Wayne, about my dilemma. He told me to write a letter to Hawks and explain myself.

In the cast was a wonderful actor named R. G. Armstrong, who had a degree in English. He helped me with the letter. I really laid it on thick.

I left the letter at the reception desk for Hawks. Days went by and I kept seeing the letter set aside for him. Finally, out of desperation, I said, "Does he ever pick up his mail?" They assured me that the letter would be in his hands.

The next day, knowing that he got it, I showed up in Old Tucson wondering what his reception would be. At dinner, he came over to me.

"Ed, thank you for your letter," he said.

"No, thank *you!*" I awkwardly responded, while practically sinking to my knees.

Everything was okay from then on.

Another memory I have of *El Dorado* involves Jimmy Caan and I walking together on the set one day. We stumbled across Wayne sitting in a chair. Jimmy began asking him questions that I knew would ignite him.

Wayne got into an uncontrollable rage. He was so angry that he began slapping his hat on his thigh. He mentioned how he was passed up on playing General Patton in the upcoming biographical film, which later starred George C. Scott.

Wayne said he would do the movie if it was done on his terms. Ultimately, the producers wanted to do it their way. I kept my mouth shut. I knew not to piss Wayne off, especially since I had just made things right with Hawks.

Wayne was a great actor. He knew his limitations. I despised him for his prejudice against liberals, but I can't ignore his immense talent.

He had an ego but not too big for his stature.

● ● ● ● ● ● ● ● ●

I worked with another legend when I filmed *The Venetian Affair* at the Doheny Mansion in Los Angeles. An aging Boris Karloff was in it. I didn't get to know him well, but I spent some time with him. I got to appreciate him and I liked him very much. In my opinion, he was typecast and an underrated actor.

Similarly, the television movie *Haunts of the Very Rich* taught me what a great actor Robert Reed was. Unfortunately, he was typecast as Mike Brady from *The Brady Bunch*. It's a shame when great actors don't get the recognition they deserve because the audience can't separate the actor from the character. He was a compelling actor.

Between movie roles, I steadily did guest appearances during the late 1960s. I did multiple appearances on *The F.B.I.*, *The Invaders*, *Ironside*, and *The Name of the Game*, each time appearing as a different character. I also appeared on *The Wild West* and *Mission: Impossible*.

They Call Me Mister Tibbs was my second encounter with Sidney Poitier, after *The Slender Thread*. It was the sequel to *In the Heat of the Night*. I played a real estate salesman who somehow got in too deep.

I remember that I wore actor Lee J. Cobb's wig during filming, at least that's what the label said. I looked ridiculous in that thing. Poitier used to tell me, "Take off that wig!" I guess I could be in a much higher place in Hollywood if I wasn't a hitching post for outlandish wigs.

At least Cobb didn't have head lice…

It might sound odd but my first *real* break was not working with John Wayne, Elvis Presley, or Boris Karloff, but the 1970 television movie *House on Greenapple Road* starring Janet Leigh.

The movie was intended to be the replacement for *Perry Mason*. I played Sheriff Muntz. He was a schmuck and kind of buffoonish. It wasn't very good, but my performance in the movie attracted the attention of MTM Enterprises cofounder Grant Tinker.

So, there ya have it. I put in the time and paid my dues to the industry. I worked long hours without much recognition, but I persevered and look back fondly at those roles. I learned how to play the game and rarely was without work. I grew as an actor during this time, which helped prepare me for the role of a lifetime.

CHAPTER 9
OH, MR. GRANT

"Can Ed Asner do comedy?"

Prior to cofounding MTM Enterprises, I think Grant Tinker worked at 20th Century Fox in some executive position. After seeing my performance in *House on Greenapple Road*, he recommended me to *The Mary Tyler Moore Show* creators Jim Brooks and Allan Burns.

Jim Brooks was quirky and Allan Burns was a Steady Eddie. James created *Room 222* and Allan cocreated *My Mother the Car* and *The Munsters* before creating our show.

This early *Mary* promo, dated June 2, 1970, are some of the first shots of me as Lou Grant.
Photo courtesy of CBS

Following Tinker's recommendation, they asked Ethel Winant, vice president of talent at CBS, "Can Ed Asner do comedy?" And she said, "Ed Asner can do anything." She believed that I wasn't working as much as I should have been.

To this day, I don't know why Ethel supported me, but she dug me. I think casting director Marion Dougherty felt the same way.

Well, how the story goes, Jim and Allan were still hesitant about my ability to do comedy. They watched me on an episode of the political drama *Slattery's People*, starring Richard Crenna, but that made matters worse because my character was very serious.

Luckily for me, one of Grant Tinker's close friends was Richard Crenna. Grant supposedly told him how Jim and Allan were struggling to cast Lou. He said, "They don't think Ed can be funny." Richard responded, "No, he is funny. He really can be funny. You oughta see him." Because of Richard's recommendation, Grant insisted that Jim and Allan audition me.

So, they reluctantly brought me in to read for Lou Grant. It was the scene from the pilot where Lou hires Mary. I remember looking at it and thinking, "Oh, this is good shit." So, I did my best and read for them.

"Well, that was a very intelligent reading," Jim said.

"Yeah, but it wasn't funny," I thought.

"We'll have you back to read with Mary," he said.

That's a good sign, I thought.

Everything felt very polite between the three of us so I couldn't gage whether they really liked my reading or not. Jim told me that he wanted me to read in a wild, all-out, crazy manner when I came back to read with Mary. I said, "Uh-huh, uh-huh, sure." I had no idea what he was talking about.

As I walked out of the audition building, I somehow got the courage to go back in and say, "Look, I'm not sure what you mean. Let me try it that way now. If I don't cut it, then don't have me back." I still don't know where that gumption came from, I had never talked like that before and haven't to this day. I'm lucky I did though because I've heard that my audition was so bad that they were considering not bringing me back.

Jim said to me, "Well, we do have another appointment." From what I've heard, I believe the next audition was with Gavin MacLeod, who also auditioned to play Lou Grant. Can you imagine? Gavin playing Lou? I've never heard a mean word come from that man's mouth!

So, they let me read the scene again and I did it like a real *meshugana*. I didn't know what the hell I was doing, I was saying, "Mary," pronouncing the

My stories are really boring. Can you tell?
Photo courtesy of CBS

a as *ay*. I was really stressing the *ay* to them. I sounded crazy, but they laughed their asses off.

"Read it just like that when you come back with Mary," they said.

What the fuck did I do? I thought. *How* did I do it? *Why* were they laughing?

I was tortured for the next week or so until my reading with Mary. I had no idea what I did for them or what they found funny. My stomach was in knots the entire week.

So, I came back to read with her. I tried my best to be as *meshugeh* as possible. And, they laughed again! I couldn't believe it!

In her autobiography, Mary described our reading together "like a scene from *Silence of the Lambs*." She likened me to "Hannibal Lecter with an intense appetite for Jodie Foster's liver." I always thought of Lou as a lady killer.

Even with her lovely take on our reading, I got the part.

A couple years later, I found out that after I left the audition room, Mary turned to Allan and Jim and said, "Are you sure?"

"That's your Lou Grant," they responded.

● ● ● ● ● ● ● ● ●

We shot the pilot on a dumpy stage over in some Hollywood studio. The place was leaking and had low ceilings; everything was in horrible condition.

I was enthusiastic about the show, but it wasn't until I read the second or third script that I realized how special the show truly was.

Our writing was amazing. Stan Daniels was a staff writer on the show. He had the demeanor of an old rabbi. He was very funny. He used to do an old routine with a Yiddish accent. Ed Weinberger came on board years later with experience working for Johnny Carson. The show had incredible writers.

Jay Sandrich, or "Relentless Jay" as I called him, was brought in to direct the pilot. I found Jay to be a real pain in the ass. He was telling me what to do, and I didn't agree with his direction. I was confident that the show would sell and, with my grandiosity, I thought, *Well, okay, I'll buy him for now, but once we get on the air, I'll do my best to see that he doesn't come back.*

In our second or third year, cameraman Bill Cline witnessed an argument between Jay and me. Bill said to Jay, "Look, Ed might let you win if you don't make him lose his temper anymore." Jay responded, "Five will get you ten, we'll have lunch together," which we did.

The problem was that we were both very outspoken. Thankfully, my ego didn't get the best of me. We found a middle ground and Jay went on to direct the series.

I remember that jealousy certainly played a factor in my resentment. Jay spent a lot of time with the girls, Mary, Cloris, and Valerie. I remember feeling pissed off because the boys, Gavin, Ted, and me, were left wandering in the woods. It was frustrating at the time, but as each girl left to do her own series, Mary was forced to spend more time with us, and they had the scripts written that way.

I guess the writers were learning all the time how to write for women. And, that's why I came to respect Valerie and Cloris, in their own *meshugana* way. We'd be going along and we'd reach a point where the girls would say, "I can't believe I'd say this, or I'd do that." They really stood up for themselves, and Jay would say, "Well, show it to the producers and then we'll work it out." Nine times out of ten, they'd make the modifications in the writing.

●● ●●● ●●● ●●●

We eventually became one big happy family. We all had our strengths and played off those strengths to support each other. Our cast was like no other.

You will never find another show where the actors meshed together as well as ours did.

Mary Tyler Moore was a magic maker. We would be working our asses off on a scene and then we'd break for lunch, which generally turned into a two-hour lunch. And, she would use that time to take a dance class.

That's who Mary was, an incredibly hard worker. She wanted to be a dancer more than anything in the world, and that mentality turned her into such an effective actress. I never had a problem with her. She was a straight arrow.

After the show ended, I felt that Mary changed. She did a couple of things, which left me feeling rejected. One example of this is when my son Matt and I had somehow obtained permission to produce the release of *Mary* on DVD.

While trying to interview people involved in the show, I naturally turned to her. I told her that Matt wanted to interview her for the bonus features. She said no.

I don't know if she had someone else that she wanted to produce it, but she refused to do the interview. I don't think she ever did it, but what he put together was wonderful.

This early Mary promo, dated June 2, 1970, are some of the first shots of me as Lou Grant.
Photo courtesy of CBS

There was a reunion gathering a few years back. I remember that I was about to sit next to her and she said something like, "I'm glad you came, I wouldn't have."

I don't hold any ill will toward Mary. She gave me my big break. I envied her. I was jealous of her drive and her natural acting ability. She was the consummate professional.

● ● ● ● ● ● ● ● ● ●

Valerie Harper came to the producers' attention during casting. Paul Sills had done a play using fairytale characters and she was in it. They wanted her badly and she came in to play Rhoda. She was wonderful.

She bewitched Mary early on, who found Valerie to be funny and charming. That didn't help with my jealousy at the time because she certainly was the darling of the company. It went on that way for years, as Mary and Valerie.

As time went on, Valerie's agent was getting restless, so after a couple of years, they gave Valerie her own show. She was sorely missed, but we still saw her through guest appearances, either on her show or ours.

● ● ● ● ● ● ● ● ● ●

Cloris Leachman was the belle of the ball. She was always fun. We used to hang around all the time. We were both pros and we knew it. We could appreciate value when we saw it.

One story I have about Cloris occurred while we were preparing for the show. It was determined that I would go to Chicago and do promos for a certain number of cities with Mary. And then I would go to Atlanta and do the other half of the list with Cloris.

So, not having done this before, I memorized everything for the promos. Well, I got to about the second or third promo and my brain just wiped out. I couldn't retain it. Also, I didn't want to use my glasses so I couldn't read the cue cards. Mary ended up taking the load. I was humiliated.

I got to Atlanta and I let Cloris know how I fouled up in Chicago. She told me, "Look, we don't need this shit, we can do our own." So, we did improv and we had a lot of fun. And it was good. She restored my confidence and passion.

We used to get real chummy and jokey with each other. One day, we were sitting in a car talking.

"Well, I'll tell ya what. You lose thirty pounds and we'll do it," she said.

"Hmmm...Yeah?"

So, I lost twenty-nine pounds. Either that last pound was the hardest to lose or I stopped at twenty-nine out of fear. I'll never know whether she was joking or not, but that was her sense of humor. She didn't act like she was willing to settle for twenty-nine though.

It wasn't meant to be.

● ● ● ● ● ● ● ● ● ● ●

Ted Knight was the funniest man I ever came across. Watching him walk with his duck ass sticking out made you want to laugh. We were very close. Ted, Gavin, and I would go out for dinner every Friday night.

I remember a time when Ted was doing a scene without Gavin or me. So, we were walking through the stage, and he said, "Listen, I want you to look at this scene I'm doing. I'm going to try it a different way." Gavin and I had already watched the scene and laughed our asses off, but we said, "Okay, we'll watch." It was just as funny, different, but just as funny.

Then Ted said, "All right, I wanna try it a third way." We said, "Okay." And it was almost as funny.

So, finally, what he chose was the first method with modifications, but it was beautiful and funny. I'm sure Gavin and I both thought, *You son of a bitch, we struggle to make it right the first time, yet you give us three variations of the same scene and show us how easy it is.*

● ● ● ● ● ● ● ● ● ● ●

Gavin MacLeod is a wonderful, warm, and loving creature. He's very supportive and always found something to laugh about with Ted. He would find things to laugh about with him even when I wouldn't see the humor.

He had already found fame before *Mary* with the movie *Kelly's Heroes* with Clint Eastwood. As I mentioned earlier, he auditioned for the role of Lou Grant. At the time, Allan and Jim thought he was a better fit for Murray. I am glad they could see his immense talent, beyond his Lou Grant reading, and hired him because *Mary* wouldn't have been the same without him.

Gavin holds a special place in my heart. When I had problems with my wife, he provided support for the both of us. He was there for my wife and he was there for me. I am extremely grateful for my relationship with him.

● ● ● ● ● ● ● ● ● ● ●

Betty White is one classy broad. She was funny and great to work with. She really inspired the writers to write well. And, she has never refused anything I've asked of her. She's wonderful that way.

Sue Ann Nivens was the perfect role for Betty: strong, smart, and sassy. I remember one episode where Sue Ann convinced Murray to be her stooge. She dressed him in a bridal gown that she was designing.

The whole group was appalled with what she was doing to him. Murray, finally having enough, picked Sue Ann up and sat her down on a wedding cake.

I remember hearing Betty's tuchus hit the wood board where the cake was sitting. It made a loud *thump!* She must have been hurt but continued the scene. She said, "It could use a little lemon!" That proved to me what a pro she was.

●●●●●●●●●●●

Working on *Mary* was seven years of joy and being with people I loved. Seven years that went *way* too fast. The show taught me a lot about life and acting.

I learned how to *do* comedy.

I learned how to *judge* comedy.

I learned how to *evaluate* good writing.

I learned what it was like to be part of a unit.

Everything I learned from *Mary* was because I was surrounded by people who sacrificed for each other, rather than for themselves. I was surrounded by a talented, caring, and funny group of individuals. *Mary* made me a household name. But, looking back, I'm much more grateful for the lasting friendships and relationships it gave me.

CHAPTER 10...
CAN ED ASNER DO DRAMA?

"Why do you grimace so much?"

When *The Mary Tyler Moore Show* was coming to a close, I was unsure where my career would take me. I had just spent seven glorious years on a hit sitcom. Did I want to pursue movies? Another sitcom? Take a break?

Luckily, the feeling of uncertainty didn't last long. CBS had a show in mind for me, one that felt comfortable.

Immediately after the network announced that *Mary* was ending, I learned that CBS wanted me for a spin-off. They even told me that I could pick a producer for the show. I chose MTM Enterprises and my two producers from *Mary*, Allan Burns and Jim Brooks.

After about a month or so, Allan and Jim came to me and said, "We think we want Lou to go back to his origins, print journalism. We also think it should be an hour-long show." I was so naive, but said, "Whatever you guys want, yeah. You're my tutors. You're my guides."

So, they prepared an hour-long show for my character Lou Grant. I wasn't sure how the format would work, but I had immense confidence in Allan and Jim.

Leon Tokatyan wrote the pilot. He was a brilliant writer. And, the interesting thing was, nobody connected with the script had ever done an hour-long show. They'd done half-hour shows and movies, but nobody had ever done a weekly hour-long show.

I was extremely nervous of this undertaking. I played Lou for seven years, but never as a dramatic character. I had experience as a dramatic actor but not in morphing the same character from comedy to drama. I think the image of my two brothers, Ben and Labe, guided my approach, along with the encouragement of Allan and Jim.

As the pilot started shooting, I noticed all the differences between filming a sitcom versus a drama.

Labe, Ben, and me.
Courtesy of Asner Family Photo Collection

We went from a three-camera setup with a live audience of 300 where I looked for a laugh wherever I could get it to a single-camera show, where there's nothing but silence.

Even though there were laugh lines in *Lou Grant*, you couldn't laugh. The crew couldn't laugh. I realized the value of the comedic lines in our scripts, as they were interspersed in the drama. We didn't want to waste those laughs.

I'll always remember, during my first day on the show, my kids were on the set exploring. We were busy filming and the cameraman yelled, "No! No! No good! There is a kid walking around in the background!"

So, I looked around and there was my daughter Katie! I asked her, "You came through that door while we were filming?" And, she pointed at one of the adult extras and said, "Well, he did too!" I guess the acting bug skips a generation.

When the show debuted, I was in therapy. I remember lying on the couch after the show opened. I rarely asked my therapist a direct question because he was Freudian.

"What did you think?" I inquired.

"Why do you grimace so much?" he said while looking at me.

Right then, it hit me like a ton of bricks. I thought, "Oh my God." He was right. I guess I was grimacing to indicate the laugh lines to the people watching at home. After that, I immediately wiped the grimace off my face and kept it off.

So, we soldiered on, but people were confused by what the series was about. *TV Guide* listed the show as a comedy for the first two episodes. The *Los Angeles Times* even featured a picture of me on the cover of its Sunday television section, which read, "Ed Asner in a New Comedy." It eventually got straightened out and people began to realize that the show was an hour-long drama.

As the show went on, I became in *Lou Grant* what Mary was in *The Mary Tyler Moore Show*. She was the axle. She was the hub around which everyone revolved. Allan and Jim would remind me of this constantly. Like I was the ringleader and everyone waited to follow my lead.

I remember, Bud Grant was the vice president of programs at CBS Entertainment, and he had a big party at this place in West Los Angeles. At the time, the numbers weren't great for the show.

I said to Bud, "God, I'm so worried about this. You know, getting the show done...," and he said, "Don't worry, if this doesn't work, we'll do something else." I remember thinking, *That's great, he sees value in me, but I don't wanna hear that.* I wanted my show to succeed.

Evidently, CBS thought we were wasting my character's potential on a boring newspaper show. They actually requested that Lou be more like Kojak and start hitting people. I guess they thought that all bald men are angry and picking fights with people.

So, we kept doing our best, and since CBS had nothing else waiting in the wings, we were renewed for a second year. And, the ratings slowly improved. We were a modest success.

The fantastic scripts kept coming in the second season. I remember looking at them and thinking, "That old Lou is not going to work here. He can't operate out of these scripts. I can't perform them, I can't execute them."

I said to myself, "I can't use my brothers anymore to help develop this character. I've got to find some new inspiration." And, I did. Lou became me.

As time went on, I became more and more myself in Lou Grant. I actually found that this version of the character was more like me. He embodied more of my personality than he ever did on *Mary*. I learned that what I needed to do was supply the bulk of the character more effectively, rather than grimacing and striving for laughs. It freed me.

Thankfully, I was surrounded by great actors who helped my character develop. Without their help, I likely wouldn't have been able to transition from comedy to drama so smoothly.

Robert Walden was feisty. He exhaustively prepared himself for his work. I had great admiration for him. Linda Kelsey was beautiful and also did a great job. They both worked long hours on the show, much longer than I did.

Linda was not originally cast in the series. Rebecca Balding played our female reporter. However, the producers felt that Rebecca wasn't working well so they replaced her after three episodes.

At the time, Rebecca was dating actor Bruce Davison. And, one day, he came down to the set and wanted to demolish producer Gene Reynolds for firing her. I liked both actresses. Linda was just different than Rebecca.

Mason Adams was perfect. I really thought that he was impeccably cast and incorporated everything into his character. He helped me feel relaxed in my role. I enjoyed him.

Nancy Marchand was the greatest actress in the world. Somewhere along the way, maybe midway through *Lou Grant*, her character, Mrs. Pynchon, hired an efficiency expert to see what could be done to expand the paper.

So, toward the end of the episode, the time comes where she has to make a decision and she calls us into her office to tell us what she had decided. Well, Nancy had this speech that they wrote for her and in that speech you know which way she's going to go.

Her brilliance was evidenced by each time she did it. First the master shot, then a two shot, then over the shoulder, and then a close-up. Each time she did it and went through that speech, you became less certain of what she was going to decide.

By the final close-up, I was in awe. It was not until she got to the final line of her speech that you could decipher her decision. And, to me, that was the greatest proof in the world. She had to be the best actress that ever came down the pike.

Jack Bannon was a stud. Initially, I met him and was not taken aback by his acting strength. But, in the first year, there was an episode involving his character's dying mother. Watching him do the scenes, I realized what unbelievable depth he had as an actor.

Darryl Anderson had the unattractive chore of portraying every photographer that ever inhabited a newspaper. He played it from the sleaze

The last show of a great run.
Photo courtesy of CBS

angle, and I watched him grow as an actor throughout the run of the show.

I didn't think *Lou Grant*, being a drama, could mimic the magic from my *Mary* days, but I was wrong. Obviously, both shows had different approaches, but when great writers come together with talented actors, the result is exhilarating.

Who'd have thought this grimace could become the face of a leading man?

CHAPTER 11
"THE JANE FONDA OF LATIN AMERICA"[1]

"It was a slight goof, an honest mistake."

While shooting *Lou Grant*, I became increasingly frustrated with my union, the Screen Actors Guild (SAG). My interest in unions stemmed all the way back to my auto plant days in Chicago.

I vowed never to work at another auto plant for as long as I lived. My experience at GM and its open-shop union was a nightmare. However, the hourly rates at Ford, which was a closed-shop union, drew me back in.

The stark contrast between the two auto plants convinced me, over all else, that I was a union man forever.

With SAG, I found that the presidency was based on who you knew in Hollywood. New blood rarely appeared. I considered myself a liberal, but above all, I was a staunch union man. Ensuring that SAG took care of its members was more important to me than politics.

A proud member of my union.
Courtesy of SAG-AFTRA

---

[1] This chapter's title derives from a nickname given to me by a conservative group, as featured in *New York Magazine* on March 15, 1982, with the headline "What Does Lou Grant Know About El Salvador?"

I had a lot of liberal friends at the time, including Kent McCord, Marvin Kaplan, and Ron Soble. All of whom, for the most part, were outsiders. They were not considered as potential SAG office holders. However, we all agreed that SAG leadership was in dire need of a shakeup.

Once I achieved celebrity status with *The Mary Tyler Moore Show*, *Lou Grant*, and *Roots*, a large number of union outsiders approached me to run for SAG president. Time after time, I refused. I was political but still very hesitant to put myself out there. Maybe I was nervous that I would lose if I ran. I'm not sure.

Sometime later though, SAG was going through a tough TV/theatrical strike under President William Schallert. I was even on the picket line fighting for better rights. The 1980 strike stretched from July until its conclusion in October.

I personally felt that the strike concluded too swiftly without enough advances for members. To end the strike, Schallert agreed to allow cable television stations to broadcast shows for ten days before being required to pay residuals to the actors.

I was very critical of Schallert's handling of the strike. That's when my mindset changed. I wanted to help my fellow actors and fight for their rights, which I felt Schallert failed to do. So, when I was asked to run this time, I said, "Sure."

Speaking in solidarity to my fellow actors.
Courtesy of SAG-AFTRA

I ran on the platform that SAG should merge with the American Federation of Television and Radio Artists (AFTRA) and the Screen Extras Guild (SEG). I also fought hard for better working conditions and ending unemployment for SAG members.

I wanted SAG to play a part, not just in the lives of actors, but in the labor movement as a whole. Many of my opponents felt that I was trying to make SAG too political.

The following is a sample of my campaign promise, in my own words, or at least what SAG-AFTRA's website claims to be my words:

> I have no magic solution for the problems facing the Guild but, if elected, I will totally dedicate myself to enhancing our identity as proud workers and unionists.
>
> To strike out at the attitude that the performer is not a worker.
>
> To enlighten the performer who feels guilt at success and divorces himself from his peers.
>
> To work toward that unity of performer unions wherein all artists will feel strength in numbers and freedom from jurisdictional squabbles.
>
> With these accomplished, the two contracts we face by 1983 will be satisfying realities. We are family.

I miss Bill Schallert and Patty Duke, who once played father and daughter. Bill preceded me as SAG president, and Patty succeeded me.
Courtesy of Ray Bengston/SAG-AFTRA

I had no idea whether I would win or lose, but I defeated William Schallert by a vote of 9,689 to 7,188. He was a good man, but a lot of members found him to be too indecisive. I came into SAG ready to fight and expecting to be more decisive than he was.

Supposedly, I was the first person elected president without any prior experience as a board member or officer of SAG. It was also the second time that the nominating committee chose a new candidate over an incumbent seeking reelection.

Evidently, I was the right man for the job.

I didn't know what was in store for me as president. I was working ten-hour days on the set of *Lou Grant* and then was expected to run a union of nearly 50,000 members.

Actress Mariette Hartley must have been a psychic because, after my victory, she sent me a congratulatory telegram.

"You put me on one committee and I'll deck you," it read.

A few years later, I realized that she knew something I didn't. If only she would have warned me before I decided to run.

● ● ● ● ● ● ● ● ●

My first years as SAG president were certainly polarizing. Many opponents felt that I was too liberal and had a personal "vendetta" against Ronald Reagan, who was president of the United States at the time.

Negotiating with producers and studios is never fun.
Courtesy of SAG-AFTRA

Working with Dennis Weaver was a pleasure.
Courtesy of SAG-AFTRA

I think this started when our board of directors decided not to give Reagan SAG's top award. A committee recommended that Reagan should receive the award, but the board of ninety-nine members voted against it.

I believe that many people attributed that decision to me. Like, I personally persuaded the board to vote against Reagan. SAG's spokeswoman claiming that the vote represented SAG's disapproval of Reagan's societal concerns didn't help the situation either.

Reagan and I obviously had differences, but I wasn't on a crusade against him, contrary to what many conservatives suggested at the time

I'm proud to be a part of SAG.
Courtesy of SAG-AFTRA

([*cough*] Charlton Heston [*cough*]). I didn't agree with his foreign policies. But, more importantly, I didn't agree with his anti-labor sentiments.

Reagan was an actor himself, who championed labor unions early in his life. He was even a former SAG president. I felt like, after attaining the highest office in the country, he was turning his back on his friends.

During my entire presidency, it felt like there was a liberal/conservative divide between actors. There were my supporters and there were Reagan supporters. Burt Lancaster, Jack Lemmon, and Carroll O'Connor continued to support me, while Charlton Heston, Clint Eastwood, and Barbara Stanwyck maintained support for Reagan.

There was no in-between. It was me or him.

My SAG-AFTRA-SEG merger proposal was narrowly defeated, I think partially because of the political divide. Heston believed that the merger was an attempt on my part to obtain more power, rather than my real motivation, to strengthen SAG's bargaining power with Hollywood producers.

Celebrating my fellow actors.
Courtesy of SAG-AFTRA

Heston and I constantly sparred in the news. I would make a statement, he would respond. He would make a statement, I would respond. It became a weekly dance between the two of us. I actually started to enjoy our rivalry, wondering what the *schmuck* had to say each week!

So, that's how my presidency started. Perhaps I was too political, but members knew that about me when I was elected. I was outspoken and I didn't want to disappoint my supporters. I took stands that I believed in, regardless of how it made me look, because I truly believed it was in the union's best interest.

● ● ● ● ● ● ● ● ● ●

During the fifth season of *Lou Grant*, we were really hitting our stride. Our scripts had relevant societal topics and the cast was never better. No one thought we would make it past our first season, nonetheless make it to a fifth season.

The show had won several Emmys, including two for Outstanding Drama Series, four for Nancy Marchand, and two for myself. I was incredibly proud of our show because we overcame increasingly difficult odds to succeed.

Playing the same character differently.
Photo courtesy of CBS

My schedule was jam-packed at the time. I was starring on the hit drama while also moonlighting as SAG president. I received a great deal of attention within the industry. I was expected to be a leader both on and off the set. I can't say I was fully prepared for that responsibility.

During this time, El Salvador was in the midst of a civil war. A revolutionary guerilla group was attempting to overthrow the government. President Ronald Reagan's administration promised not to get involved. However, the United States became entangled in the war and eventually assisted the Salvadorian government.

A Catholic nun named Sister Patricia Krommer approached me. Thinking of me as a decent human being, she thought I would help her by attaching my name to the Archbishop Romero Relief Fund, which was established to take care of refugees from El Salvador.

She gave me literature and showed me a Dutch documentary featuring death squads and corpses lying in the streets of El Salvador. I was outraged thinking that the United States was partially responsible for it. We were sending them guns and empowering the Salvadorian leadership by placing their top army officials in the School of the Americas.

Not too long after that, Bill Zimmerman came to me. He had created a medical aid fund for Indochina and had been very successful there. Now he wanted my help to generate medical aid for El Salvador.

Traveling in style.
Courtesy of Asner Family Photo Collection

He came to me and said he wanted me to join the board of directors of the Medical Aid for El Salvador organization. He planned to go to Washington, DC, after the first of the year to announce the formation of the association and present a check for $25,000 to a group of Mexican doctors.

I said, "Okay."

So, the time came for us to go to Washington, DC, and make the formal announcement. Bill Zimmerman came, along with actors Lee Grant, Howard Hesseman, and Ralph Waite.

There I was on the steps of the State Department, the SAG president, the largest actors' union in the country, reading the preamble to our relief organization. Cameras were everywhere. Pictures of me handing over the check would later follow me wherever I went.

After the announcement, we had a press conference scheduled at the Capitol Hilton. When we got there, we went into this room, which was packed with reporters. And, because I was the star of an ongoing television series and probably recognized by most, I stayed up there and started taking questions.

The first question was a pop fly, easy. The second question was by a cable news reporter. He asked, "You said you're in favor of elections in El Salvador. What if those elections create a communist government?"

Right there, it hit me.

How was I going to answer this question? I was scared shitless. So, I mumbled some lazy answer and moved onto the third question.

However, I was troubled by what I just did. I thought, *You've come all this way, and now you're going to piss it away?* I felt like I had to provide him with a straight answer.

I gave a quick response to the third question and turned back to the second reporter.

"I wasn't happy with the answer I gave you," I said.

"What I'd like to say is, if it's the government they choose to have, let them have it."

And just like that, I felt like my career was over.

After the press conference, I found myself sitting in a room. Columnist Mary McGrory said to me, "How did you feel about that assemblage out there?" And I said, "What did you think of it?" She said, "I thought they were hostile."

So, I waited for the shoe to fall. My answer haunted me. It was tearing me up. I wondered about the fate of my show and whether I would be labeled as a communist.

All this torture, based on *one* answer.

During the controversy, I received death threats and even hired private security. Posters labeling me as "Communist swine" covered the SAG headquarters in Hollywood. A recall petition was circulating to remove me as the SAG president.

An anti-Asner rally, led by Charlton Heston, was held at the North Hollywood High School auditorium with Mike Connors, Dean Jagger, Don DeFore, and Robert Conrad all in attendance. Heston motivated the crowd with "promises of support from Jimmy Stewart, Clint Eastwood, Alan Young, Jonathan Winters, and Irene Dunne."

Even with all this drama, I continued to respond to the verbal attacks. "It was a slight goof, an honest mistake," I said. I also clarified that my statements were as an individual and not in my capacity as the SAG president. Unfortunately, that didn't go over well.

One of the producers of *Lou Grant* came down to see me one day to try to talk some sense into me.

"There are two ways of dealing with the problems that we deal with," he said.

"There's the way you deal with it, and the way the show deals with it."

"And I think the show's a better way."

What did he want me to do? Roll over and take the attacks? The damage was done. Sponsors were dropping left and right. Kimberly-Clark, Vidal Sassoon, and Cadbury Chocolate all ceased their sponsorship of our program.

A couple of congressmen were even calling for a boycott of the show. Charlton Heston was practically lighting torches and buying pitchforks. News commentator Bruce Herschensohn was essentially breaking down the door so that my adversaries could come in.

I was lost. I felt like I was captaining a sinking ship that I couldn't maneuver.

During this time, I started hearing stories that *Lou Grant* was in trouble. So, I called Arthur Price, who was running MTM at the time, and he reassured me that the show was fine.

"Ed, I was just at CBS," he said.

"If I had a sense that it was in trouble, I would have fought for the show."

A week later, *Lou Grant* was cancelled by CBS due to a "sharp decline in audience response."

People ask me all the time whether I think the show was cancelled due to the El Salvador controversy. I still, to this day, wholeheartedly believe that was the case.

At the time, the show was averaging a 27 share and a 16.6 rating. This was only slightly down from the 32 share and 19.6 rating we averaged the three prior seasons.

The network obviously felt pressured because sponsors were leaving and their leading man was a so-called "communist." I've heard stories that William Paley, the president of CBS, insisted that the show be cancelled, but I don't know if there is any truth to that.

Do I feel guilty about what went down? Yes and no.

I feel guilty for the cast and crew. The show was *good*. It deserved a lot better. Hundreds of people, *talented* people, were out of jobs because I couldn't keep my big mouth shut.

On the other hand, I am proud for standing up for my beliefs. Maybe my ego got the best of me while I was the SAG president, but I said what I said because it's truly how I felt. During the entire controversy, when I was attacked, I responded. I didn't run. I didn't hide. I stood up.

Years later, my agent, Jack Fields, who did a lot for blacklisted actors, said "I thought your career was over." He said, "What saved you is the fact that you kept fighting back."

"I think that's what saved you," Fields said. Maybe, but I certainly was in for the biggest fight of my life.

CHAPTER 12
ROCK BOTTOM

"I needed all the friends I could get, and he sacrificed me."

Boy, oh, boy, the 1980s sure started off with a bang. I went from the top of the Hollywood heap to the bottom of the "Communist" barrel. I had starred in a hit sitcom for seven years, received a spin-off that lasted five seasons, was elected SAG president, and won seven Emmy Awards.

Now, nobody wanted to hire me.

People I worked with for years and admired acted like I was the walking plague. They avoided me and were afraid to be seen in public with me. The mere utterance of "Ed Asner" was considered career suicide.

I remember when *Lou Grant* got cancelled; my agent was busy looking for work for me. He went to Jim Brooks and said, "It's been difficult to find Ed work." And, Jim supposedly responded, "Yeah, I think he's been too political."

Ted Knight, whom I adored, had a press event for his show *Too Close for Comfort*. And, he made comments like, "*Lou Grant* was boring," and, "They used Ed." I needed all the friends I could get, and he sacrificed me.

I was officially blacklisted in Hollywood.

I've never been at a place in my life where I felt so alone. I felt completely isolated from the world. At that time, Martin Sheen took out two full-page ads in *Variety* and *The Hollywood Reporter*. He ended the ads with, "Ed Asner, you are not alone."

If only I felt that way. And, to make matters worse, Nancy and I were separated at the time.

I have always been universally regarded as a flirt. I was during my youth. I was while preparing to be an actor. And, I was when I achieved celebrity status.

Unfortunately, I was a flirt when I was married. Actually, I was more than that.

I was a *cheat*.

It isn't easy to admit and it certainly isn't easy to write, but it's the truth. When I was married to Nancy, I cheated on her. I cheated on a woman who adored me. I cheated on a woman I adored. I cheated on the mother of my children.

Nancy gave me everything I could ask for in life: love, passion, and three beautiful children. But, I desired more. You can call it needy. You can certainly call it selfish, because that's what it was. I failed her.

I was infatuated with women. Nancy would satisfy my needs, but it was never enough. My eyes would always be drawn to women. I think Nancy had suspicions, but we never discussed it.

This went on for years and I couldn't tell you how many women, but I was restless and decided it was time to tell her. She deserved to know the truth. For some reason, in my naive mind, I thought my confession would be greeted with absolution.

It wasn't.

I approached her as a very depressed individual. She asked what was wrong and I told her that I wanted a break from marriage. I actually had the nerve to ask Nancy for permission. To my surprise, that ignited the trail to divorce. She asked me to leave.

I moved into the house across the street, which we recently purchased. I figured, I would enjoy myself for a few months and then I would win Nancy back. Guess, who was wrong?

Nancy filed for divorce. My longtime assistant later said that she would testify against me in court. She must have noticed my behavior in the office and around other women. The funny thing is that I don't blame her. I actually wanted someone in Nancy's corner because I certainly didn't deserve it.

The divorce haunts me to this day because I still love Nancy. I always will. I wish I could have been the husband she deserved. She was there for me as a struggling actor, she moved with me to California so I could pursue my dream, she put up with me during filming, and even consoled me during the El Salvador controversy, but it wasn't enough for me.

I remember the first time I met her, at the dinner with Jerry Orbach and Frank Perry. She was the most beautiful woman I had ever seen. I made a grand gesture by bringing her flowers to her hospital room. A part of me wishes that another gesture like that could win her over again. Like magic, *POOF!* and all the pain I caused her would be erased and that she could look at me again like she did at that steak dinner.

Life doesn't work like that though.

If I'm such a good actor, why couldn't I act like a better husband? That's the one role I haven't been able to pull off. I'd take a Husband of the Year Award over an Emmy any day.

Nancy, I'm so sorry.

● ○ ● ● ● ● ● ● ● ○

Every day after *Lou Grant* was cancelled was a struggle, my home life was in disarray and I desperately needed *another* big break. My livelihood relied on guest appearances, voice roles, and made-for-television movies. I took small supporting roles simply for the paycheck because no one would hire me for a lead role.

To be perfectly honest, I didn't think my blacklist years stretched as long as they did until I started writing this book. There were years when I would only perform in a handful of projects. My ego certainly took a big hit.

I know of one instance where I was, for sure, blacklisted.

There was a medical show, I believe named *Ryan's Four*, where writer Howard Rodman said, "Ed would be great for the role of the older doctor." The producer responded, "No, I think he would be a political liability." The role eventually went to Nicolas Coster or Tom Skerritt.

The funny thing I learned about being blacklisted is that both sides take a part in it. I knew my El Salvador comments would infuriate the right-wingers, that was inevitable. But, I was shocked to learn that even liberals, people I thought shared my beliefs and values, refused to cast me.

With many conservatives, I was blacklisted because I was a so-called "commie." With liberals, however, I wasn't blacklisted for being "too political." I was blacklisted for being "overexposed," "too fat," or "too old."

Liberal producers did not want to blame my politics so they looked for other explanations. The reason for this is because, even though they may have agreed with my views, they didn't want me to kill their project.

Producers knew that with me being attached to their production, half of the country would refuse to watch. They would then also be associated with a "commie" and their project might fail. No one wants their project boycotted.

Looking back at it, I understand their reservations, but I needed someone in my corner. I also can't help but think, if I had a friend who was in a similar situation, would I help them? I'd like to think I would. So, even though I understand it, it still hurts that no one would fight for me.

● ● ● ● ● ● ● ● ● ●

Finally in 1985 I got a lead role on the sitcom *Off the Rack*. Eileen Brennan and Dennis Haysbert costarred. It was a good show, but because there was a writers' strike at the time, we never had a shot. The network only aired six episodes before it was cancelled.

A couple years later came *The Bronx Zoo* on NBC. I played the principal of Benjamin Harris High School. I thought it was a decent show, but I felt that executive producer Gary David Goldberg didn't fight for us enough. We were renewed for a second season, but it was cancelled after twenty-one episodes.

Off the Rack and *The Bronx Zoo* were the only substantial lead roles I had during the 1980s. I'd have a voice-over role here, a video short there, but roles were few and far between. The 1990s were not much different.

JFK might have been my first big role while on the blacklist. I got to work with a man I adored and admired, Jack Lemmon. He was a great guy who supported me during my SAG days. I think I got the role because director Oliver Stone pitied me. But, who could blame him? I pitied myself at that point.

Stone treated me very well. He was always open to suggestions from his actors and improving the script. While filming, I knew the movie was something special. Stone's direction, cuts, and angles were out of this world. In my opinion, he was robbed of the Academy Award for Best Director.

I'll always remember pistol-whipping Jack Lemmon during a scene. The gun was made of rubber, but I guess I hit him pretty hard because he started bleeding. I felt horrible because I adored Jack. Stone asked if he wanted to take a break, but the consummate professional that he was, Jack kept going.

With each scene I was more and more careful not to hurt him, but it didn't look real. So, Jack kept telling me, "Come on, Ed! Make it look real! Take a good swing this time!" Yeah, okay, but that didn't stop him from making me feel guilty later. Evidently, he had ringing in his ears for a week after shooting, even though he told me it lasted for a *month*. What a little shit! I miss him.

What surprised me the most about *JFK* was how much praise I received for my performance. I expected that people would say, "There Ed goes again, another one of his conspiracy theories." But, no. People would stop me and say how surprised they were with my performance. It felt great.

Around this time, I started to find success with cartoon voice-over roles. I starred in *Captain Planet and the Planeteers*, *Batman: The Animated Series*, and *Spider-Man*. I don't know what stud was the physical inspiration for my character Sgt. Mike Cosgrove in *Freakazoid!* but he was one beautiful follicly challenged man. These roles were nice, but it wasn't the same as being in front of a camera.

In 1994, I gave sitcoms another chance. *Thunder Alley* costarred Jim Beaver and Haley Joel Osment, pre–*The Sixth Sense*. I played a retired race-car driver whose grown daughter moves in with him. We fared well during our first season because we were paired with *Home Improvement*, but our ratings dropped off significantly during the second season. As a result, we were cancelled.

What really stands out to me about the show is how frequently we recast the role of my daughter. First, Felicity Huffman played my daughter. She was then replaced with Diane Venora, who was then herself replaced with Robin Riker. It was a regular game of musical chairs on that show.

Then came *The Closer*. Working with Tom Selleck was a delight. The show proved to me that I was actually capable of getting along and working with a Republican.

The series likely would have gone on longer, but I think Selleck and CBS President Les Moonves were at odds. We only shot ten episodes, but my favorite episode involved my character getting high off pot brownies. I kissed actor Steven Gilborn square on the lips!

● ● ● ● ● ● ● ● ●

So, that's how the 1980s and 1990s went. They resembled the days when I first arrived in California trying to make it as an actor. I was happy to get any job. I had some decent roles, but many failed projects.

Being blacklisted is an interesting thing because no one prepares you for it. Acting teachers instill techniques and motivation to be successful in the industry. However, once someone achieves success in Hollywood, no one can tell you how to navigate through fame.

Being a "celebrity" is a personal experience. Some people can handle it, some people can't. Some actors can play the game for years and be universally liked by all. Others burn out or just don't have the knack for being in the public eye.

I never learned how to play the Hollywood game. I took political stands. I overindulged. I spoke when I shouldn't have. These are mistakes that celebrities, who want to be loved, probably shouldn't make.

I, on the other hand, thought it was better to be myself. I lost work and the woman I love because of it. Was it worth it?

CHAPTER 13...
PICKING MYSELF *UP*

"He looked exactly like Paul Douglas, the former senator from Illinois."

All of my children have been there for me, through the good times and the bad. Matthew, Liza, and Katie are all grown now, and I couldn't be more proud of the people they've become.

Matthew has held executive positions with Autism Speaks and the Autism Society of America, which has led him to the task (with his wife Navah) of creating the Ed Asner Family Center. Liza, after earning a degree in broadcast

My son and his boys.
Courtesy of Asner Family Photo Collection

One of my twins, Liza, had her own!
Courtesy of Asner Family Photo Collection

journalism and running various arts and music programs here and in Oregon, became my booking agent/stage manager. Katie, after being a graduate herself and a working actress, is now a marriage and family therapist.

They are all winners and give me boundless joy. They took after their loving mother Nancy and overcame their father's bad habits. Thank God!

However, I'd like to believe that the one trait they got from their schlub of a father is the strength to fight for the little guy. Each one of them is a caring and devoted individual. I wish I could have been half the parent each of them is today.

After my divorce from Nancy, I had a second son, Charlie, with my girlfriend. He came twenty years after my last child was born. I wasn't expecting to be a father again in my late fifties, but Charlie was a bright spot during a very dark time in my life.

I am incredibly proud of him. He is on the spectrum and a graduate of Southern Connecticut State University. I had the honor of speaking at his graduation and handing him his diploma (just like I did at Liza's ceremony). I attribute his success, in large part, to my ex-wife, Cindy, who certainly played a major role in his rearing.

Twins are twice the fun and twice the love.
Courtesy of Asner Family Photo Collection

He is a good kid and the key reason why autism awareness holds a special place in my heart. Prior to his diagnosis, I will be the first to admit that I didn't see the warning signs. He was an average high-energy rule-breaking kid to me. He struggled in school, but it wasn't until he was six or seven that we realized testing was necessary.

While Charlie was growing up, not many people knew about autism or what caused someone to be on the spectrum. We didn't have the knowledge that we do today. Thankfully, we found a good public school and worked our butts off to get him the help he needed.

Anyone can be affected by autism. I also have a grandson who is on the spectrum. But what people don't realize is that if someone is diagnosed with autism, that doesn't mean the person can't live a normal life. They can hold full-time jobs, get married, and have children, just like anyone else.

Being autistic holds a certain misguided stigma in society, especially in the workplace. Many employers are afraid to hire people who are on the spectrum. It has been a goal of mine to generate a greater understanding of who autistic people are and what they can do.

Nancy with Matt and Liza.
Courtesy of Asner Family Photo Collection

Katie and her family.
Courtesy of Asner Family Photo Collection

Autistic individuals can be some of the brightest and hardworking people. They just need a chance. Charlie has thrived when people have accepted him and seen his endless potential. I'm thankful he educated me on this important subject that affects one in nearly seventy children.

I guess being outspoken for a cause can be good at times.

• • • • • • • • • •

In the late 1990s, I was always looking for charitable causes to fill my time. My work schedule was still wide-open so when political activist Bob Schwartz approached me, the timing was perfect.

Bob contacted me to take part in a medical relief delegation, which included Muhammad Ali. He wanted us all to travel to Cuba, along with aid groups Disarm Education Fund and Direct Relief International, to deliver medical supplies to children who needed them.

My youngest son's graduation. So proud of Charles.
Courtesy of Asner Family Photo Collection

I was still feeling the sting from being blacklisted so I had nothing to lose. It was for a good cause and I am not the type of person to turn my head on the less fortunate based on a country's political views.

At that time, the embargo was obviously still in effect between the United States and Cuba, which greatly hindered the Cuban government's ability to obtain medical supplies. To this day, I still do not understand how any country could allow an embargo to limit proper health care for children.

So, I embarked on a three- to four-day trip to Cuba. I was fascinated to learn that very few people recognized me. This was due to the limited access of American television in Cuba. But, everyone recognized Muhammad Ali and cheered his arrival. I suppose I was in good company.

While there, we toured hospitals and clinics. We delivered $1.2 million in medical equipment and supplies. Muhammad, who was suffering from Parkinson's disease at the time, was an inspiration. He performed magic tricks during the trip, and even played a little basketball. I saw him make a three-point shot.

On the last day of the trip, Cuban President Fidel Castro surprised us with an appearance. He called our donations a "great moral gesture." However, he seemed far more interested in Muhammad Ali than me. I, of course, was the signer of all the letters that brought the supplies to Cuba, but whatever, I wasn't jealous at all.

Okay, *maybe* a little.

Meeting Castro reminds me of a story. I had a friend who did on-air reporting for NBC. He went to Harvard during the same time Castro visited the campus in 1959. So, when he met Castro at breakfast while on assignment in Cuba, one of the first things my friend brought up was how he used to go to the same bar Castro visited during his trip. Castro wasn't impressed. He completely ignored him.

Then at lunch, my friend saw Castro again and mentioned the bar for a second time. Still, no response from Castro. Then dinner came and once again, my *overly* persistent friend mentioned the bar *again*. This time, Castro erupts with all kinds of excitement and stories of the nights he spent there.

Two men of history and me.
Courtesy of Emiliano Thibaut

My friend was in shock that Castro ignored him twice before only to have fond memories of the bar. He then mentioned Castro's response to a Cuban official. He asked, "How did that happen?" And the Cuban official said, "Oh, you weren't talking to Castro at breakfast or lunch. Those were his body doubles." The first two guys were doubles! I wonder if he held a Jack Lord–esque audition for his back too…

Now, I sit here and wonder if I actually met Castro or a Castro lookalike.

Either way, the trip was a massive success and it felt great to provide aid to children who desperately needed it. I expected some backlash from my critics, but, hey, they were already calling me a "commie." So, why did I care? The trip was not political in any way; it was strictly for humanitarian purposes. I'm proud to have taken a part in it.

Lonnie Ali, Muhammad's wife, described the trip perfectly. She said, "Regardless of whatever political problems we may have with the country of Cuba, its people are just as human as we are, and we feel a need to reach out to them."

● ● ● ● ● ● ● ● ● ●

I think it took twenty years for my name to officially come off the blacklist. Not until *Elf* came along in 2003 did I finally feel that my career was revived. It was ideal. Jon Favreau guided us well, and I loved the story. I knew the movie would become a holiday classic.

Will Ferrell was brilliant in the movie. His comedic timing was perfect. It was so much fun to do, and I loved the version of Santa Claus that I was hired to perform. He was a regular guy. My Santa could take Edmund Gwenn's Santa in a brawl any day!

A few years later I did the movie *The Christmas Card*. Its popularity shocked me. I had done many television movies in the past, which didn't fare as well. People still write

Perfect role for a nice Jewish boy.
Licensed by Warner Bros. Entertainment Inc. All rights reserved

me about the movie to this day. It had a great story and became a holiday classic of sorts.

I costarred with veteran actress Lois Nettleton, who played my wife. She was very disoriented during filming. She would ask the director, "Where am I?" The director would say, "In the script?" And, she would respond, "No, where am I now?" It made me very sad to see her in that condition. She was a talented actress and a sweet woman. She passed away shortly after the film aired.

Then came the second role of a lifetime, Disney•Pixar's *Up*.

I was picked out of the blue. My voice-over agent submitted me for the part and directors Pete Doctor and Bob Peterson came and saw me in a reading of Emilie Beck's wonderful play *Number of People* in Alameda County. The subject matter for the play was very serious. I played a Holocaust survivor suffering from dementia.

I didn't know they were there at the time, which was probably for the best because I didn't have the opportunity to try and impress them. Luckily, they decided to hire me after that performance. It still amazes me that Carl came from such a depressing story. I think it was the tragedy of my performance that clinched it for them.

I loved the *UP* team.
Courtesy of Deborah Coleman/Pixar

So, I prepared for the role like I did for any other voice-over. I always worked alone while reading for Carl. I was pleased to hear around the third or fourth session that the animators were thrilled with the variety I was giving them. I got a note which said, "Thanks for giving us so much to work with." I was delighted.

I remember seeing a sketch of Carl early on, probably during my first or second session. I thought, "My God." He looked exactly like Paul Douglas, the former senator from Illinois. He had the same big ears and white hair as Douglas. Evidently, Spencer Tracy was the inspiration.

One memory that I will never forget while recording, I was running late from lunch one day so I hurried back. I didn't see a curb in the sound room so I accidentally tripped over it. I came crashing against a wall and splitting my head open.

As I lay there in a daze, I knew that I was bleeding behind my left ear, where my head had hit. I was then rushed to the hospital. I got around five or six staples in my head and then went back to work the same day. I don't have much to damage there anyway.

The whole movie made me feel reborn. It has such a powerful message. It talks about mourning for a period of time and then living the life you're given; not letting a single moment escape you. Pete Doctor and Bob Peterson were brilliant storytellers.

Pete and Bob were great collaborators.
Courtesy of Deborah Coleman/Pixar

Jonah Rivera is a class act.
Courtesy of Deborah Coleman/Pixar

To me though, I must give immense credit to producer Jonas Rivera. He really helped me develop Carl. His support throughout the entire process made Carl possible and I can't thank him enough for his guidance.

Jordan Nagai also deserves credit for his performance as Russell. Supposedly, Jordan came in to the casting call with his older brother, who was auditioning for the role. However, after hearing Jordan in the waiting room, the casting agents asked him to read. I don't think he had ever done that before, but they chose him over his brother. I was totally amazed that they got that kind of performance from him.

The funny thing about *Up* is that I spent years trying to break free from voice roles, only to have one of my greatest performances be a voice role. During my blacklist years, I was always striving to be in front of a camera, to be a lead actor again, but *Up* really connected with its audience.

People felt an emotional connection to my character, I think because everyone has lost someone in their life and been unsure how to cope with the pain. Carl showed that life is worth living and that we all can get second chances.

Up was my second chance, and I am extremely grateful for it.

Since *Up*, I've been making my rounds with guest appearances on television shows and some movie roles, but I've primarily found myself being drawn back to the stage. I did off Broadway in Chicago with Playwrights Theatre Club and in New York at the Theatre de Lys, but I've also found success on Broadway.

I had a minor role in *Face of a Hero* with Jack Lemmon in 1960, starred in *Born Yesterday* alongside Madeline Kahn in 1989, and more recently *Grace* in 2012 with all-around good guy (which I have to say because he wrote the Foreword to this book) Paul Rudd.

I was hesitant to take on Broadway again with *Grace* because my previous attempts were not that successful. But, the cast and director reeled me back in. Paul Rudd and Michael Shannon are real pros. We had a blast. The rehearsal process at age eighty-two was difficult, but director Dexter Bullard was very capable of handling our massive egos (especially Paul's, talk about high maintenance!).

I also toured the country in my one-man show *FDR* from 2009 to 2015. I was able to play my hero and, in my opinion, the best president this country's ever seen, Franklin Delano Roosevelt. I know what you're all thinking, the resemblance is uncanny! And, you're right. We both liked sitting down and neither of us knew how to say goodbye to a role we liked.

Most recently, I've been touring with my one-man show *A Man and His Prostate*, which was written by *Mary* writer/producer and comedy genius Ed Weinberger. I like to think of the show as a man's response to *The Vagina Monologues*. The show is brilliant and I owe all the credit to Ed. It's based on his true story of experiencing prostate trouble while on vacation in Italy. And I'm also playing "God" in *God Help Us* by Samuel Warren Joseph and Phil Proctor where I moderate a debate between a liberal and conservative pundit. God is pretty angry about what's been going on down here.

People ask me all the time, "Are you ever going to retire?" And I tell them that acting is what keeps me alive and kicking. If I didn't have acting, what would I do? Play mahjong and watch reruns of *The Golden Girls*? (Sorry, Betty.)

Why should I retire? I enjoy acting and it pays the bills. Anyone who has been divorced before knows that those bills *have to* be paid. A popular saying goes: *I'll rest when I'm dead*. I wish that were true, but I don't think that applies to me.

I have a feeling that when I'm reunited with my family in Heaven (which does exist, *right?*), my brother Labe, the little bastard that he was, will have some taunts and goads to make up for. Hopefully, my skin doesn't bruise so easily up there.

And, you know what? That actually sounds heavenly to me. We've got a lot of catching up to do. I just pray that Charlton Heston isn't waiting at the Pearly Gates to greet me…

CHAPTER 14...
ODE TO THE JUNKMAN

"I will always be that Kansas City Jew you raised."

As I sit in my office right now, writing this final chapter to my autobiography, I see two Emmys sitting on my desk. To the left of them, there is a large picture of my father at his junkyard hanging on the wall.

Every time I find myself looking at the Emmys, I can't help but turn to that picture of my father because it reminds me of who I am and where I come from.

Many people use awards to justify their existence or demonstrate a sense of self-worth. However, I use them to remind myself of my roots, my upbringing, and the people who helped me get to where I am today: my mom, my dad, my siblings, even Nancy and my children.

The Emmy Awards!
Photo courtesy of CBS

At eighty-eight, several things haven't changed over the years:

I'm still that Kansas City hick looking for approval from his father.

I'm still that average Joe struggling to make ends meet at the auto plant.

I'm still that hopeless romantic looking to be loved.

There is a well-known saying: *You can take the boy out of the country, but you can't take the country out of the boy.*

Truer words were never spoken. Being an actor is no different from growing up in the West Bottoms of Kansas City.

I struggled in my early years, working as an encyclopedia salesman, a spot polisher at an auto plant, and at my father's junkyard. I was always fighting for a paycheck and looking for that big opportunity.

As an actor, the struggle was similar, first in Chicago, then New York, and then California. I paid my dues by working in the theatre, doing bit parts, and making guest appearances for little pay before I made it big.

I've always felt like an outsider. Being one of the few Jews in Kansas City, I was blackballed from a fraternity in high school and rejected by a girl I liked because of my upbringing. Similarly, I was blacklisted in Hollywood because of my political views and being outspoken.

If I could give one piece of advice to all the young actors out there it would be: *Be true to yourself.* Before you become an actor, know who you want to be in life and stick with it. Fame can do a lot of things to you, but if you are true to yourself, you will never look back at your life with shame.

I have many regrets during my life. Especially when it comes to the way I treated Nancy. I will never outlive that guilt. But, when it comes to my career, I can undeniably say I am proud of the choices I made.

I think back to that time in the Playwrights Theatre Club and the backlash Paul Sills received for screening *Salt of the Earth*. I voted against the screening because I cared more about my career than taking a stand for what I believed in.

Today, I see that young actor as a coward. He didn't speak up when he should have. I am grateful I learned to be true to myself and speak up, even though it cost me a great deal of work.

I hope when my family reads this book, they see a fighter, someone who fought for his principles and never backed down. I inherited that virtue from my father. He was rough and unapologetic. He held me and my siblings to a very high standard.

I still hold myself to that standard.

ODE TO THE JUNKMAN 93

Courtesy of Asner Family Photo Collection

Lou Grant was more me than on MTM.
Photo courtesy of CBS

When I look back at the controversy I created during that press conference in 1982, I think my father would have been proud of me. I didn't do what was popular, I did what I thought was right.

My dad always fought for the little guy. If he was still alive, I'd like to believe that he would have been on those State Department steps with me or at least in the audience cheering me on.

My father died in 1957, long before he could see me starring on *The Mary Tyler Moore Show*. I think that has been the main driving force in my life. My dad never saw me succeed. He didn't see all those years in Chicago pay off. When he died, I was a college dropout chasing an impossible dream.

After I dropped out of college, I called home and told my sister that I was planning to visit Kansas City. My father relayed the following message to me: "Tell him that if he couldn't make it in school, he's not going to make it as an actor."

I wanted his approval so badly, but I wasn't able to get it. He saw me fail at my bar mitzvah and at Judaism, but he didn't see everything I accomplished. He died before he could meet Nancy. He didn't see me accept my first Emmy from Lucille Ball and Jack Benny. He didn't get to meet my wonderful children.

After he died and I achieved some success, my mother pulled me aside and said, "I want to tell you that we were wrong, and I'm glad." It felt good to hear those words.

I've achieved a lot in my life. And, I don't take a second for granted. I owe everything to the three groups I thanked during my acceptance speech at the 1971 Emmy Awards: the family I come from, the family I made with Nancy, and my *Mary Tyler Moore* family. Without them, I'd just be another pretty face.

Dad, I hope I made you proud. I will always be that Kansas City Jew you raised. More importantly, I will always be the son of a junkman.

Love, Eddie.

AFTERWORD

I first met Ed Asner in 2001 when he agreed to participate in a staged reading of a play I wrote entitled *Moral Imperative*. It was an extraordinary evening to hear my words performed by him. And it wasn't until that night I realized that Ed was not just a television star, but a world-class actor. His ability to combine humor and pathos in every moment of the performance was a sight to behold. The intelligence and nuance he demonstrated was breathtaking, and this was just a reading with only one rehearsal!

I lost touch with Ed until a few years later. After a session of the Actors Studio Playwrights/Directors Unit of which I'm a member, I found a note on my front windshield that said, "I dented your car. Call me. Ed Asner." And he left me his phone number. I hadn't seen Ed there, but I was happy to be able to make contact again. The next day I called him; he had forgotten who I was and the amazing reading he did of my play. He offered to get the dent fixed. It was minor, so I said, "Take me to lunch instead." He did, and we've been friends ever since.

It says something about Ed that he left that note. Most people aren't that ethical, but Ed wears his ethics and morals on his sleeve—and it has cost him. It cost him a television series and probably opportunities he should have and could have had. As a political and union activist, he has not shied away from taking controversial positions. Ed Asner cares about fairness and justice for those who are abused and less fortunate. Simply, there are few celebrities who have consistently advocated for progressive causes as Ed has. There's a Yiddish word for Ed. He's a *mensch*, which means "a person of integrity and honor." Leo Rosten defines a *mensch* as "someone to admire and emulate, someone of noble character." His life is a testament to that word.

This is not to say Ed doesn't have his warts and flaws, but he is unfailingly candid about those.

Ed's career spans from the Golden Age of Television to today, and I was surprised that nobody had written his biography. Ed told me that there had been some attempts, but nothing came of them. Ed is a great storyteller and I thought an interview book would be a great format to tell his life story. It took some convincing, but Ed finally agreed. He sat down for a series of interviews in the summer of 2017, and the result was the first draft of the book, an oral autobiography that includes key moments of Ed Asner's life and career, a career that included performances with the top actors and directors of the last sixty years—including Paul Newman, Sidney Poitier, John Wayne,

Mary Tyler Moore, Sidney Lumet, John Ford, Sidney Pollack, and on and on.

However, to me, as much as I loved the show business parts of the book, the sections about his family and growing up as the youngest of five in a family of entrepreneurs and hustlers were eye opening.

Ed decided he preferred a more traditional autobiography written in prose format, and Matthew Seymour did a terrific job working with Ed to reshape and rewrite the book you just read.

However, there was so much material, we have decided to include some of the actual interviews to fill in the gaps, so to speak. The following "Additional Interviews" are like the bonus features you find on a DVD.

Ed Asner has been part of America's television living rooms, movie theatres, and stages for over sixty years. His performances have moved audiences to tears and made them laugh hysterically. His political activism has been dynamic, inspiring, and consequential. He is a father and a grandfather devoted to his children and grandchildren. His is a remarkable life that we are honored to help share with you, the reader.

—Samuel Warren Joseph

P.S.—I want to thank my former student, Ani Margarian, for her excellent transcriptions of my interviews with Ed. And most of all, I want to thank my beautiful wife, Sandra, for her incredible support and help throughout this entire endeavor.

ADDITIONAL INTERVIEWS

SAM: Did your Uncle Frank (Lizzie's brother) make a living street fighting or was he just a tough guy?

ED: Tough guy. So if the bohunks made fun of my grandfather's beard, he would beat the shit out of them.

SAM: Oh, really? Did they make fun of him because he was Jewish?

ED: I guess the beard was distinctively Jewish at that time, so they did. He was a man of peace, but a later story, which I just heard a couple years ago from my brother, was that my grandfather lived on the Missouri side, and come Pesach, he'd make wine, and I don't know if he sold it or gave it. But evidently, prohibition was in effect at the time, of course.

There's the story of one of his neighbors over there, found out he was making the wine, so he approached him and said, "You gotta give me some money so I don't squeal." Well, my grandfather was terror stricken, couldn't believe it. He was a scholar, a Yiddish scholar. So, he told my mother. My mother told my father. And my father said, "Don't worry. I'll take care of it." So he was due to come by the next morning to my grandfather. So, I never knew of my father to be a brawler either, but evidently, come the next morning at dawn, Dad got in his car and drove to the Missouri side, parked around the corner, walked to the house, went in, and told my grandfather to lie low. He'd handle it. So, the neighbor came by sometime later, knocked on the screen door, and said, "Hey, Seliger," my grandfather's name, "You got my money?" And I guess my Dad mumbled something, "Come on in," he beat the shit out of him. [*Sam laughs*] He said, "Yeah, is that enough money?" Never heard from this neighbor again.

SAM: [*laughing*] Have you ever decked anybody?

ED: No.

SAM: When's the last time you were in a fight?

ED: A real fight was—the only fight, really, was in the Army. This guy was nothing but a fucking crab, bitched *all* the time. Nothing—nobody was good, nobody was decent. They all trashed on him. So, I verbally challenged him. I said, "Well, you wanna fight?" And this was during a break on learning radar. And he says, "Yeah." So he gets up. I've never fought in my life. So, we squared around, and, all I know is wrestling, basic grabbing and holding.

So, I grabbed him and was wrestling him around and he said, "Ah, you chicken shit, you don't wanna fight, huh?" And I thought, *Oh, this shit*. So, I shoved him away and I put up my dukes and we started swinging at each other. I think I scratched his nose. And then finally the corporal in charge of us broke it up. I thought it was pretty comical myself at the time. But, a couple other guys there were evidently bothered by this shithead. And they thanked me.

SAM: Oh, that's good. Because you know, in a sense, it's interesting. You were a football player, right? An athlete. You were strong.

ED: My father's junkyard made me strong.

SAM: Right.

ED: And his genes.

SAM: And his genes. But fought your whole life, in a sense, for what you thought was right, but you never were violent?

ED: No. Well, other people thought I was violent. I guess it's the shadow I cast.

SAM: Yeah, I think people might perceive it, but you're not violent.

ED: No. I like puppies.

SAM: You like puppies? [*laughs*] Okay.

ED: I like little, little kids.

SAM: You said earlier that your father used to build houses.

ED: Now, he had rudimentary knowledge. Somebody would have a leak, and he'd take a goddamn board, and he'd pound it in, and the leak would be fixed.

SAM: You said that they lived in houses that he built.

ED: Yeah, shacks, whatever.

SAM: So, he did build these little shacks?

ED: Yeah, well, he took them over. I'll put it that way.

SAM: And he rented them out?

ED: Yeah.

SAM: I see. But he primarily owned a junkyard.

ED: Primarily, solely. Frank and my uncle Morris had both gone out on the road as, what'd they call them? Salesmen?

SAM: Traveling salesmen?

ED: Drummers, drummers. I think they called them drummers.

SAM: Drummers?

ED: Traveling salesmen. I think Frank finally opened a junkyard in, ended up in, what'd they call it? The panhandle of Texas.

SAM: Right.

ED: Border Texas. A really roughhouse place. He set up a junkyard down there. "Pipe and supply" was what they would call it. And, while he was down there, Morris went farther south and he eventually started a cotton ranch.

SAM: Cotton ranch?

ED: Yeah. Cotton and grapefruit. And, well, he lived a nice life too. Didn't have any kids.

SAM: Neither one had kids?

ED: No. Well, no, Frank did. Frank had two boys.

SAM: Are they still alive?

ED: No. No. The one about Labe's age, Labe would taunt him and bug him. Although Labe was short, he overcame his shortness by being a feisty prick. And he made mincemeat out of his cousin Louis, who further along was running after his brother Maurice, older brother. Maurice slammed the door that he was running through and the glass shattered, and he blinded Louis in one eye.

SAM: Oh, no.

ED: Yeah. So, Louis became a physical specimen. If he wanted to, he could have beat the shit out of my brother. He was a great athlete, but small… And eventually he, Frank, my uncle Frank, invited my brother Ben to come down there and work with him. So, Ben had nothing pressing to do, said, "Okay." He wasn't going to college, so he went down there. And there came a point where, well, this was prior to Ben. So there was an oil company going out of business, and Frank saw all the junk and steel they had, pipes and pumps, and this and that. And, uh, there was too big a deal for him alone. So he called my father and said, "Come in with me." My dad said, "Okay." So, so this took place in El Dorado, Arkansas, at the time I was born. So about the time he saw the puntilla. Yeah. So, they had all this oil equipment. So Frank said, "Oh, we got all this stuff. Why don't we drill?" My dad said, "Go along, get along." They drilled and struck oil.

SAM: No kidding!

ED: At that time, I can't remember the exact figures, was probably going for like $1.10, $1.30 a barrel. And, that was a good, nice going price. And then

My grandfather and my siblings and cousins.
Courtesy of Asner Family Photo Collection

one of the West or East Texas strikes came in, and there was an oil boom. And it depressed the shit out of oil prices.

SAM: I see.

ED: So what they were getting $1.30 for, maybe, plunged to $0.90 a barrel, and they went belly-up. And they sold all the equipment they could, and my mother had to pawn whatever jewels she had. And, my dad came back to Kansas City like a loser, and Mom washed bottles during the day. The bottles that we supplied the bootleggers with, Dad started making the stills. And they supplied them with chemicals that they needed, that they could buy. And corks. Shit like that. Then that went on during the time that I talked about. And, then '33 came along and prohibition was over.

SAM: And there was no money in it. So, what did they do after that? After prohibition?

ED: They had a junkyard.

SAM: Still had the junkyard.

ED: Yeah.

Tight as a drum, ready to die for my country. (Those holes are on the photo, not the wall.)
Courtesy of Asner Family Photo Collection

SAM: Does that junkyard still exist?

ED: Oh, yeah. Labe's son-in-law Buzzah runs it now.

SAM: Oh, it's still in the family?

ED: Yeah.

SAM: Oh, no kidding. What's it called?

ED: Asner Iron and Metal.

●●●●●●●●●●

SAM: Didn't one of your brothers own a record store or something?

ED: Yeah. It's called Capers Corners.

SAM: Capers Corners.

ED: Cause he liked to raise Dalmatians.

SAM: Which brother was this?

ED: Ben.

SAM: Ben. Ben was closest to you?

ED: No, no. Labe was.

SAM: Labe was.

ED: Yeah. He was six years older than me.

SAM: He was the one who just passed.

ED: Yeah. He's the one whose pinch would bruise me, and tease me and tease me, tease me.

● ● ● ● ● ● ● ● ● ●

SAM: Did Morris have brothers?

ED: Oh, yeah. That's his brother in that picture.

SAM: Okay.

ED: That brother…this was on the Lithuania…Belarus border. Well, that brother I can't remember what his name was. Anyway, he came over before the war.

SAM: Right.

ED: My father came in the late 1800s, late 1890s. But, this brother came over and joined him in the junk business. Stayed a few years, I guess got lonely or wanted his wife, if he had one, decided to go back to Russia.

SAM: I see.

ED: He then sired. What did he sire? Six boys and a girl. The girl was close to the eldest. Became like a second mother to them. The youngest boy was kind of a cripple. And in the middle were five brothers. I can't remember their names. Abram *(sic)* was the only one that survived. The oldest brother lived in a separate shtetl from the family when the Germans came in.

SAM: In Russia?

ED: Yeah.

SAM: The Germans came in during—

ED: World War II. The invasion of Russia.

ED: Oh, I know. Well, he went back. And, I don't know if they… I don't think they were alive by then. By the time of the German invasion. But the older brother lived in a separate shtetl. And the four healthy boys, including Abram, saw the German occupation in their shtetl and they put a rough barbed wire wall around it. And, the four boys didn't like the smell of it. And they decided to escape into the woods. People were already escaping into the woods. The—

SAM: So these were your first cousins?

ED: Yeah.

ED: And the...the cripple, it would have been too arduous for him to go with them. So the older sister elected to stay in the village with the cripple. By the end of the war, they were gone. The brother who lived in a separate shtetl was gone. And the four boys, during the course of the war, formed their own partisan band.

SAM: Oh, really? So they were fighting the Germans?

ED: Yeah. And their fame reached enough of a celebrity that they were called "Yitzhak's Boys." So, that brother was called Yitzhak, which is my name as well.

SAM: Oh, is it?

ED: Yitzhak. Isaac.

SAM: Isaac. Did Yitzhak survive the war?

ED: No. One of the brothers was killed by a German, another by a Pole—third committed suicide rather than taken prisoner, so that left Abram and the wife he brought with him.

SAM: So, they lived here—

ED: No, they settled in Canada. Windsor. And he primarily worked for Chrysler while he was here. He just died at ninety-something a year or two ago. She died before. So that's here in the States. My father had a sister who ran a dairy farm, big as a house. Tremendous bones on these people. [*Sam laughs*] I mean, goddamn it. Big sons of bitches.

SAM: Big people?

ED: Yeah, very big.

ED: Asna (*sic*) was her name.

SAM: Asna?

ED: Yeah. She ran the dairy farm. And, she had two kids. Helen and Ben. And Ben was a big [*laughing*] son of a bitch. I mean, you'd look at him...concrete would be easier to go through.

SAM: Wow.

ED: And he was a fullback.

SAM: Really?

My Dad at work with my uncle. The junkyard is still in business today!
Courtesy of Asner Family Photo Collection

ED: At, the agricultural the high school. And he was good. And Helen was something of a beauty. Ben never had any kids that I know of. But he had a sense of humor. He would always make—

SAM: This Ben you're talking about is your—

ED: Cousin.

SAM: Cousin. First cousin?

ED: Yeah. But, if he had a mean bone in his body, he could have made kindling out of my brother Ben. But he never tried. But he was a monster, as I recall from my lower position.

SAM: Yeah, from being a little kid.

● ● ● ● ● ● ● ● ●

SAM: There's more about Ben I wanted to talk about. He was shot at one point.

ED: Oh, yeah.

SAM: Who shot him?

ED: A hold-up guy.

SAM: Where?

ED: Ben had such a checkered career, it's unbelievable.

SAM: Talk about it.

ED: Well, eventually went down to Texas to be with my mother's younger brother, Uncle Frank, and run his Panhandle pipe and supply.

SAM: Right, you mentioned that before.

ED: Yeah, so, he's down there and they were found to have in their possession equipment stolen from Phillips. So, there was a big conversation between the lawyers and my uncle, and Ben, he decided it would be best if Ben took the blame.

SAM: So, Ben went to jail?

ED: He was sentenced to Huntsville Penitentiary.

SAM: For how long?

ED: He was there a year. I don't know how long the sentence was. He finally came back and he was drafted, or joined, I forget which, in World War II.

SAM: Did he fight?

ED: No. He was ferrying planes.

SAM: I see.

ED: Came back and married a shiksa. It was hard on my folks, of course, my dad, especially. He served in Texas, I guess, I can't remember where else. And, he finally came out. He came out. He was a scrambler, as I said. They needed a cardboard container for their boxes. So, he'd buy cardboard from my dad and from other places, and he'd take it to a local box company and get it cut to size, and sell it. So, that gave him his initial gelt. And from there he moved more into selling surplus; he'd locate surplus and sell it, out of my dad's place for the most part. And then he'd rent it to this guy and they built houses in what became one of the nicest suburbs in the city, Johnson County. He built his own house at the same time, moved into it. Ben, because he was operating a concrete block plant, a cinder block plant, big fucking plant and supplying most of the buildings in the area, and going to Vegas and having a great time. Then, because he paid *his* creditors, the various homeowners who bought his blocks, et cetera, weren't paying him. So, he eventually went bankrupt.

SAM: Oh, no.

ED: Oh, yeah.

SAM: So, he had started businesses, he went bankrupt, but he was always a hustler, he was always entrepreneurial.

ED: Oh, a hustler, yeah. I mean, he had sold shoes when he was younger and all that.

SAM: You didn't tell me how he got shot.

ED: I'm about to tell you.

SAM: Okay.

ED: So, then, trying to pick himself up, somehow already he had a deal, some guy he knew, that supposedly, when a railroad car is broken into, or has its lock broken, the stuff in it becomes available for purchase. So, I don't know whether he hired a guy to break the locks or whether he just stumbled on it, but he'd buy it. A lot of it was records and disks and recording equipment. So, he found a little shop in Johnson County and he opened his business selling records and stuff to kids. And, he went even further and arranged to—though, he didn't make any money out of it—to sell tickets to the leading rock groups coming into town.

SAM: Right.

ED: The performers. Block long lines. I'm sure everybody else was pissed off at him.

SAM: Right.

ED: So, Saturday night was the big night, of course, and he was in the shop, and he took the money from the day's profits, and drove home. They had Dalmatians that they had inside the house. As he pulled in his driveway, this guy comes up, opens the door, sticks a gun in him. My brother is so taken aback, he starts to reach in to get the money to give to him, and he shoots him.

SAM: Where? In his stomach?

ED: It chipped his sternum.

SAM: Oh, wow.

ED: And came to rest against his spine. [*Sam gasps*] So, he kept reaching for it, saying, "Money, money." And, the guy leveled the gun again, he put his hand up, shot his hand and pulverized almost every bone in the hand.

SAM: Oh, no.

ED: Yeah, he was like that. But, it saved his life. So, then the robber kept trying to get the money, the money was flying around everywhere. He started to shoot him again and the dogs were making such a racket in the house. The guy turned around and fired a gun into the garage, and fled. The car came wheeling around the corner, and he jumped into it. Well, they rushed him to the hospital. The worst part would be the hand because all the bones were smashed in there. But, they x-rayed him and they saw the bullet was right against his spinal column. And, the doctors saw that it was wavering. But, he knew he couldn't directly go in and take it, he'd probably fuck up vital parts. So, he then put him on his side, and plowed through a lot of fat on his arm, and got down to the spine, and took the bullet out.

SAM: Wow, that's great. Did they ever catch the guy?

ED: Not that I know of.

SAM: Wow.

ED: And then later, I've told you about the machine gun, right?

SAM: No.

ED: Oh, that was when he had the concrete block plant. I collected knives, so he started collecting knives. Got a big fucking collection. Then, I guess he started collecting guns, or whatever. Then, I come home from Chicago, or wherever I was, and he shows he got this Thompson submachine gun. I had already been in the army, and I said, "Wow." And he says, "You wanna try it?" I said, "Yeah." So, his concrete wall was nothing but a block of bricks. Huge wall. He says, "Go on, try it. Shoot it up." So I say, "I shot fifty-caliber machine guns, bazookas, nothing like this motherfucker." And I got the Thompson and I [*imitates machine gun sound*] and saw the bricks chipping and chipping. Such great power.

SAM: Wow.

ED: Such great power.

SAM: It's the gun the gangsters used to use.

ED: Yeah. I could've said, "Top of the world, ma," but I didn't.

SAM: What movie was that from?

ED: *White Heat*.

SAM: *White Heat*.

ED: So, then, I'll tell you about the other story about Ben is that he used to go to Vegas all the time.

SAM: Yeah.

ED: Labe would go to Vegas and he would play in the gin rummy tournaments.

SAM: Was he good?

ED: Very good. Then, I don't know what Ben would play, but finally one time, right when I first came to LA, I was doing a schlepper dicka sheriff or something, and they came to LA, and they had spent about ten days in Vegas. So, they came down to the studio to have lunch with me, or he did.

SAM: Labe.

ED: No, Ben. Ben says, "Oh, did I take them last night." I said, "Yeah? What'd you do?" And he says, "I took out ten thousand." I said, "Really? Oh, man that's something." And the thing is, he'd been there ten days, and I said, "Well, what'd you do the rest of the time?" And he says, "Oh, I lost." I said, "Oh, why'd you lose?" And he says, "Oh, there were a couple nights where I lost ten thousand."

SAM: So, he lost more than he won?

ED: Oh, of course.

SAM: Yeah, yeah. But he looked at it like, "The last night I won."

ED: I mean, he's the typical gambler, you know. "I won ten thousand on my last night." Never again. So, that's it.

● ● ● ● ● ● ● ● ●

SAM: And you have another story about Ben?

ED: Everybody.

SAM: About everybody, go ahead.

ED: Ben, my dad, and Labe, cousin Bernard, me… Who else? A guy bought a couple of tubes, and they were faulty, so he wanted his money back. And my dad said, "No, I'll let you exchange it, but you can't have your money back." And they keep going on, and on, and on, and yamming and yamming and yamming, and it got pretty heated. And Ben finally had arrived there and he listened for a moment, and he says, "Listen fella, I'll tell ya. I just want you to know that if you hit that old man, if you touch that old man, you'll leave here dead." And he looked at Ben, and they kept talking and talking. Bernard was by me with the bottles, he would be busy picking up the bottles. Bernard was not aggressive at all. And Labe, in the meantime, went in the office, got a six-shooter. And he stuck it in his back pocket—or stuck it *out* of his back pocket—and he positioned himself in a way that the guy would—at least the guy with him—would see it. The guy with him did see it, and he whispered in his ear, and he went, "Alright, give me the money or whatever." So, dad finished with him.

SAM: He didn't give him the money. He gave him the tubes.

ED: Or whatever he was posing. And he took them and he left. And Labe said, "I wanted to show him I had the gun in my hand, my pants. And I would've used it, I would've used it." So, I had two brothers who were willing to be killed for my father. And I was just busy doing my little job, wherever I was working at the time.

SAM: You were much younger than him.

ED: No, I was in high school.

SAM: High school.

ED: I could've done something. But I certainly wouldn't have been the first.

SAM: Right.

ED: But, they had their lethal capabilities.

●●●●●●●●●●

SAM: Do you remember being on *Mr. Novak*?

ED: Yeah. That was Jim Franciscus.

SAM: Right.

ED: And, what I really remember there is that I was busy doing a high school teacher, whatever it was.

SAM: I think it was high school.

ED: And, I was about to do the rehearsal and because Franciscus was the lead, they decided to do his part first. And, I remember begrudgingly doing this because they wanted to get him out in time. So, I had to work late because they got rid of him first.

SAM: Did you get overtime pay?

ED: Yeah.

SAM: You did… *Fanfare for a Death Scene*. It was a TV movie.

ED: Ridiculous, one of the few comedies I ever made.

SAM: [*laughing*] Like, except for *Mary Tyler Moore*, right?

ED: Yeah.

SAM: There was a show called *Slattery's People*.

ED: Yeah, that was a series they got me on.

SAM: And you did a bunch of those.

ED: Yeah. And, I was the Capitol Hill reporter. This was in Sacramento. We were making that pilot for that when Kennedy got killed. And, I can remember—I forget who was with me—we were all just devastated, getting the news over the teletype.

SAM: Okay. *Please Don't Eat the Daisies*.

ED: Another one of the few comedies I did. I forgot what I did. I was a teacher or something, I don't know.

SAM: *The Rat Patrol*.

ED: Well, I went to Spain for that. Albert Paulsen was the chief villain, I think. And, Betsy Von Furstenberg was his girlfriend at the time. And, traveled around with her and my wife and Al. We filmed in Al Maria. Chris George, of course, was in it. I can't remember anything.

SAM: So, you played three different characters on *The Fugitive*.

ED: Yeah.

SAM: Which I think is kind of odd anyway, because it's a series. How could they have the same guy playing three different parts, but there you go, at different times. Do you remember that show very well?

ED: There was one where I played an ex-pro ball player, and I was the muscle. Richard Anderson was the guest star—and there was a plot out to kill him. And, somehow or other, I was, I must've been instrumental in the plot to kill him, even though I was supposed to guard him. And, I wander off and I start to go nuts. I end up on a football field, and the flashbacks of me on the field, playing. And, what's our hero's name?

SAM: David—

ED: David Janssen. And he helps to save Richard Anderson.

SAM: *The Girl from U.N.C.L.E.*

ED: They brought me into the company of Stefanie, and she was cute and efficient. I don't remember what I did there.

SAM: *The Wild Wild West*. I loved that show as a kid.

ED: I loved doing it. I got on that show, Ross Martin and what's his name?

SAM: The star, the guy who plays Jim West. Robert Conrad.

ED: And, I played a sophisticated killer who's gonna kill everybody. I'm on the train with him, saying how I'm trying to squeeze money out of the United States to save lives.

SAM: I see. It's sort of holding the United States ransom, or you'll kill people.

ED: Yeah.

SAM: *The Invaders*, which was a show that I also loved. Remember that?

ED: Yeah. I had a daughter–my daughter was a beautiful girl…oh, shit. My memory is worth shit. I ran a bar, and everybody that was visited by the invaders had a string of little fingers or something.

SAM: Right.

ED: And I end up with a little finger.

SAM: So you were Invader Man.

ED: Yeah. And gotta turn it over to make it possible for them to claim more lives. I forgot how I got stopped.

SAM: Well, it's interesting, 'cause you were on it, you played two different characters on it.

ED: I did?

SAM: I've seen this some on *Law and Order,* too, where they'll use really good character actors for different parts over the years, but this was over a two-year period.

SAM: *Mission Impossible*. 1969.

ED: Martin Landau. This was one time when nobody knew what I looked like, so when they get rid of me, he could come in without any subterfuge. You got it?

SAM: Mm-hmm.

ED: So, I started working on the film. What the hell was his name? Hal. He was a producer.

SAM: I thought Bruce Geller produced it.

ED: Bruce Geller did produce it, but a line producer was Hal something. I think he had a slightly bad arm. So, I play it like I'm not tainted, and this guy, Hal, he didn't like what I was doing. Didn't like, didn't like it. So, I'm not working the next day, so they called and they said, "Can we have a meeting?" And, I come down to the studio, meet with this guy, Hal, and the director and

Bruce Geller. And we're busy talking, busy talking, and it's, you know, if I can't come across...we're gonna have to reshoot. And it's, "Oh, oh, you were made to be a bad guy. Oh, shoot." So, I went back and I played a bad guy.

SAM: But your take on it was, it was better to not reveal it.

ED: Yeah, yeah.

SAM: And they just wanted it obvious.

ED: Yeah. So, I played a bad guy, everything's fine.

SAM: Interesting. You tried to do something more interesting and they weren't interested.

ED: Yeah, yeah.

SAM: *Halls of Anger*.

ED: Yeah. I was a teacher, and Calvin Lockhart was the star, and he pissed everybody off. And, Jeff Bridges was in it.

SAM: But he was really young, huh?

ED: Yeah. That's about it.

SAM: How about *They Call Me Mr. Tibbs*. That was the sequel to *The Heat of the Night*. Who did you play there?

ED: I played a real estate salesman and who somehow got in too deep and I wore Lee Jay Cobb's wig.

SAM: You wore Lee Jay Cobb's wig? For the movie?

ED: Yeah.

SAM: How do you know it was his wig?

ED: Cause that's what it was labeled.

SAM: [*laughs*] He had worn it in another movie? Did you know Lee Jay Cobb?

ED: No.

SAM: Okay.

ED: I had a scene there where I was driving like a crazy bastard. As I figured they were about to catch me.

SAM: Did you work with Sidney Poitier, then?

ED: Yeah...he chastised me for being overweight.

SAM: Did he, really?

ED: And, you know, "Take off that wig."

SAM: *Take off that wig.* Wow. That's actually a wonderful compliment. No, really. He's saying you got the talent. He's actually being empathetic. You took it as a criticism?

ED: Yeah, of course. But, I could be in a much higher place if I didn't have (to wear) that wig.

SAM: A TV movie you were in, *The Old Man Who Cried Wolf.*

ED: This was Marty Paulson and Diane Baker, I think.

SAM: And Sam Jaffee.

ED: Yeah. I saw what these people were up to, and I tried to call attention to it, and my son and daughter-in-law thought I was having hallucinations.

SAM: Which you weren't.

ED: No. They'd bring in a psychiatrist.

SAM: So, you had a big role in this movie.

ED: Yeah. It was a TV movie, right?

SAM: Right.

ED: I think in the end I get killed because—

SAM: You know too much.

ED: —I was calling wolf.

SAM: *Do Not Throw Cushions Into the Ring,* 1970.

ED: It was a film made by my friend Steve Ihnat. It was his first film, and I played his agent. And he's playing hardball with the establishment, and I'm trying to get him to cooperate. And in the end, he implies he's not going to cooperate, so I walk away as if I'm leaving him. And he then turns around and goes back into the studio and he's cooperating. So, he made that film, and on the basis of that, was given the direction of *The Honkers*. And he was at Cannes trying to sell that show when he had his fatal heart attack and died.

SAM: Oh, no, he was young. I'm sorry.

● ● ● ● ● ● ● ● ●

So Many Roles

SAM: *Skin Game,* do you remember that?

ED: It was a wonderful movie. Lily Gossip, Susan Clarke, and our hero was James Garner.

SAM: Did you get along well with Jim Garner?

ED: Oh, yeah. I liked him a lot.

SAM: Did you know him pretty well?

ED: No.

SAM: But you worked with him on that film?

ED: Yeah.

SAM: Okay. *The Todd Killings*.

ED: Well, that's where—it's basically the Kitty Genovese killing, and I was paired with Cloris.

SAM: This is another time you worked with Cloris?

ED: Yeah.

SAM: So, you knew her pretty well prior to the *Mary Tyler Moore Show*.

ED: And I suggested that friends or brothers of mine—he would paint his wife's toenails. So I said, "Why don't I do that?"

SAM: Oh, wow.

ED: So all through the scene while she's shitting all over me while the killing is going on, I'm busy painting her nails.

SAM: You did several different episodes and characters for *The Mod Squad*.

ED: I played the owner of the circus.

SAM: Joe Walton, *Color of Laughter, Color of Tears*.

ED: I got stabbed in it. Liza saw that, and she was in her room watching—

SAM: When she was little.

ED: —when I got stabbed. She came running into the den where we were. I got killed.

SAM: [*laughing*] That's very funny. She must have been very confused. *Haunts of the Very Rich*, TV movie. Al Hunsicker.

ED: That's the one where we go to the island.

SAM: Oh, that's not *The Doomsday Flight*?

ED: No, *Doomsday Flight* is Eddie O'Brien is a mad bomber and I'm at the airport then.

SAM: Right.

ED: And Jack Lord is the FBI. I thought I was just kicking the shit out of him. And that's the movie that I profited from Leo Penn.

SAM: Right.

ED: He said, "Let's do the next one differently, differently, differently." So, I learned my lessons.

SAM: *Haunts of the Very Rich* is where you're on this island and you don't know what the hell is going on.

ED: And we all find out we're in hell.

SAM: All right. So, it's a version of *No Exit*.

ED: Yeah.

SAM: Yeah. One of the great metaphors of all literature, as far as I'm concerned.

ED: Of what?

SAM: *No Exit* is one of the great metaphors of all literature. "Hell is other people." Do you remember *The Girl Most Likely To*?

ED: Stockard Channing. Every old comic in LA at the time, and it's a great story, and I modeled myself after Inspector Clouseau, and Stockard is ugly in the beginning. So ugly, and then she has these operations done, and supposedly, she becomes beautiful, but in the meantime, she's busy killing off all the people who—

SAM: Who treated her badly.

ED: Yeah.

SAM: Was she nice?

ED: Oh, yeah. I think she did a wonderful job. I loved doing the role.

SAM: Right. So, you were doing a bunch of occasional TV movies, you did *Hawaii Five-O*. Oh, you know, that's interesting. You did *Hawaii Five-O* in 1975, and I understand you did it years later.

ED: Yeah, we connected the two.

SAM: It was the same character, right? Was a jewel thief, or something?

ED: A thief. I can't remember what he stole.

SAM: You had a big part in *Rich Man, Poor Man*. What was that?

ED: Oh, I played Axel Jordache, the father of the boys. Married Dorothy McGuire, and had my leg shattered in the war, and I'm regarded by most as a bitter cynic. What do you wanna know?

SAM: Nick Nolte? How was it working with him?

ED: He's great. He was the best actor on the set. Peter Strauss. Susan Blakely, who was marvelous, gorgeous.

SAM: How was Peter Strauss?

ED: He was fine. I haven't kept in touch with either Peter or Nick, but was honored by the Ojai Film Festival last year and had a surprise. I had asked Gregory Harrison (my son from *The Gathering*) to join us at the festival because he was in the area. Here I was in Ojai with one TV son and then my other TV son comes out to give me the award (Peter Strauss). He delivered a beautiful speech and it was special having them both beside me again.

SAM: You think they cast your part because of your fame from *The Mary Tyler Moore Show*?

ED: And I guess they had. I don't know. I'm a name actor.

SAM: Right.

ED: That's the scene where I'm busy punching the shit out of that heavy bag, talking to Peter Strauss. And I finally finish the scene, and David Greene says, "Oh my god, that was so good. Can we get rid of the plane?" And the sound recorder says, "I think we can get rid of it, but I'm not sure about the tour guide."

SAM: [*laughing*] So, you had to redo the whole scene?

ED: No, they got them both out.

SAM: Oh, did they really?

ED: Yeah. And I said, "Tour guide? I didn't hear the tour guide." And he says, "Oh, yeah." You mean, we're shooting a scene like this and you got a tour guide smack out there in someplace who's pulling this shit?

SAM: Must have gone off.

ED: No, no. To Universal, this is the money. That's where they make the money.

SAM: Who said that?

ED: The director, whoever.

● ● ● ● ● ● ● ● ●

SAM: I'm still here. So, 1976, you played Hank Cooper in the movie called *Gus*.

ED: Yeah.

SAM: Who was in that? What do you remember from that?

ED: Every comical football player you could think of, every character man in Hollywood, and a mule.

SAM: Oh, Gus was the mule, that's right. Was that the one where the mule kicks the football?

ED: Field goal kicking mule.

SAM: Was it fun to do?

ED: Not as much as I thought it would be.

SAM: Why?

ED: I don't know. I had no fun memories. Ronnie Schell was in it, he's good.

SAM: Okay.

ED: I don't know. Did it make money?

SAM: I have no idea. You also did *Police Story*.

ED: Yeah. I did a couple of them. I did the pilot, which I thought was excellent, and it was excellently cast, excellently written; Wambaugh was a big influence. Good to show cops as they hadn't really been shown before. It had a lot of ferocity to it.

SAM: So, that was a project you were proud of.

ED: Yeah.

SAM: You were in *Roots*. You played the most unlikable—

ED: No, I wasn't.

SAM: You played a—

ED: Ralph Waite was the unlikable one.

SAM: Oh, that's true. Did you know Ralph well?

ED: No, but I like him.

SAM: How did you feel being in *Roots*?

ED: Well, I had done *Rich Man, Poor Man* the year before. Battled and scrapped with the director, David Greene, to do what I did. I was very proud of it. I can't remember who the producer was of *Roots*. Oh, shit. But, uh, you can, you can find that out. (David Wolper)

SAM: Right.

ED: And I was gonna be very surprised if David Greene would tolerate me again. For instance, after I finished with *Roots*, we were still working with Peter Strauss and Nick Nolte, and they got into a disagreement, and he said something, "You're as difficult as Ed Asner." [*Sam laughs*] And Peter said, "Thank you." [*Sam continues to laugh*]. Um, so I didn't think they'd want me again for the next big thing on the horizon.

SAM: Next big miniseries.

ED: Mm-hmm. So, they did, they came back and they said, "Yeah, we'd like him to be the first mate." And I thought, "Well I'd done those characters before. I'd like to do the captain."

SAM: Yeah.

ED: Because it was a type of character that I had done very little of. Polished English gentleman. And I wanted to always branch out. So, he thought, and said, "Okay." And when I took it, I took it because I thought a lot of actors would say, "I don't wanna work with a *schvartze* (a black man).

SAM: Really?

ED: I thought that, I thought the prejudice would come forward. Shows you how warped I am. I thought I was doing a public service by shoving myself forward. Showed how wrong I was. Every actor in town had broken each other's legs to get in that show.

SAM: And you thought you were doing them a favor? [*laughs*]

ED: Mm-hmm. Yep. So, we started. And from the get-go, I hated everything. I hated the makeup girl, who gave me a shitty beard, and a shitty hairpiece. And we limped through with that. Remember filming on the beach and the sun and the moisture, the goddamn beard was peeling off on me every other minute. Always tacking it on, tacking it on. But, we did it. And what he was written as and what I wanted to portray was the good German.

SAM: Right, right.

ED: They say he was the most despicable. I took the job thinking, as the character, that I saved all those lives so that they can go on to be slaves in America. See what a good guy I was? I *saved* the lives.

SAM: So, that's how you justified it as the character.

ED: Until, at the end of my performance, I come to realize that my soul had been eaten up carrying out this mission. And the fact that Fred, what's his name? Oh, shit.

SAM: Silverman?

ED: Silverman. Had the genius of putting it on every night. Some say that it was so terrible that he just wanted to get it out as quickly as possible. But, I think he saw its value.

SAM: Yeah, it became this giant event at the time. People who don't recall this are too young, but I do—

ED: It grew, grew, grew, grew.

SAM: It was a huge event. Giant. You were on *The Insight*, I guess it was a religious show, TV series, a number of times, it says from 1967 to 1977. You played God, you played Henry, you played different characters. What do you remember from that series?

ED: Well, the one I played God in, I was especially proud. He was dressed in a shiny gabardine suit of sorts, had a bowler on. I did everything but the razzmatazz. And, they got Carol Burnett and Walter Matthau to do the Adam and Eve, and it was a very good show. So, they were only doing the show on the religious channel, but then they had the option, with the consent of the actors, to take it to broad TV. And, as I figured, Carol and Walter, did not want it released to broad TV because I was funnier than they were.

SAM: Did you work with them directly or was it—

ED: Just the three of us.

SAM: Were you funnier 'cause you were funnier, or were you funnier 'cause the writing was better for God?

ED: Well, the writing was very good. And, you know, playing it as a couple of simple tool peasants, it's not easy to be funny. But, they never said why they didn't want it to be seen on broad TV.

SAM: Broadcast TV?

ED: Yeah.

SAM: Well, I mean on wider distribution.

ED: Yeah. But I wanna promise you a good time if you happen to find out where it can be seen.

SAM: [*laughs*] I'm always up for a good time. *The Gathering*. Do you remember that movie? TV movie.

ED: Very much so. Became a cult classic.

SAM: Right.

ED: It had a wonderful cast, was a good tear-jerker, Maureen Stapleton was beautiful. I played the husband, and the kids were all very estranged. Maureen was a sweetheart. She was, oh, such a sweetheart.

ED: And funny.

SAM: Was she funny?

ED: Oh, yeah.

SAM: I never would've thought that, 'cause she seemed always so overwrought and serious.

ED: She'd wine and dine every night. Put the poundage on, that toward the end it was difficult keeping her in the dress. But, she told me that, and I will always love her for that, how great it was working with me and finding in me everything she hoped to find, and all that.

SAM: That you were everything she had hoped you would be.

ED: Yeah. I worked with Gregory Harrison on this film, as well as Bruce Davison—both of whom I still see whenever possible.

SAM: That's wonderful. Well, it was a great film. Another wonderful family film was *The Family Man* in 1979—another TV movie.

ED: Yeah, I was very proud of that too. We made it in Canada, Anne Jackson was my wife, Meredith Baxter was the young ass that I fell for. I was a bar owner, and there was a former lover who kicks the shit out of me, but it had a lot of good, good stuff in it. And, I, carrying on my own extra-marital affair, I identified strongly with it.

SAM: Did your extramarital affairs contribute to your divorce?

ED: Yeah.

SAM: How did your wife find out about them?

ED: I told her. But, I gather everybody had suspicions of me.

SAM: This one I really wanna talk about. *Fort Apache, The Bronx*, which you did with Paul Newman. Who directed it?

ED: Dan Petrie.

SAM: Tell me about that experience.

ED: It was very good. I used to go out and get drunk with the two detectives that created it.

SAM: Okay.

ED: Can't remember what their names are now, but I think one's dead. And, Rachel—shit—Philippine actress, can't remember her name. Rachel.

SAM: Rachel Ticotin. How was working with Paul Newman?

ED: It was wonderful. He was a good guy. Very good guy.

SAM: Did you know him before that?

ED: I may have met him. He supported me when I ran for president of SAG.

SAM: Oh, he did. And, how many scenes did you have with him in the film, do you remember, quite a few?

ED: Oh, no.

SAM: But you had a number of scenes with—

ED: Yeah. And I was a putz.

SAM: The character?

ED: There was a point there where I so disliked the ending where I give the "Hi-ho, the Merry-oh speech," and nobody called my bluff. So, I said to the director and to Paul, or somebody did, that I had a feeling for a different ending. He comes in and he turned his badge and I give him a big speech about how he's needed out there to stop this and to stop that, and he begrudgingly takes it and goes off to chase a rooftop thief. Well, I say, "This rings so badly for me. I'd like to have him come in there and try to turn his badge in." And I give him some bullshit that, finally, he turns around and he says, "Okay, I'm gonna turn it in. I wanna keep this. I'm gonna keep this. I'm gonna watch you like a fucking hawk. And we'll see that you never create a situation where people kill each other as we've seen in this district. We've done this and done that, cops throwing suspects off the tops of buildings. When I do see it, I'm gonna report you."

SAM: Paul Newman was to say this to your character? And that's what you thought should have been there. What happened? They didn't do it. That's a much more interesting ending.

ED: Oh, yeah.

SAM: That's a good idea.

ED: And—

SAM: You know what they should have done? They should have shot both and tested both.

ED: 'Cause I didn't do it with brio. I was apologizing all the way, and if I had believed in it to the extent that I believed in it and sold it that way, I might've gotten an audience. I mean it's a well-liked movie anyway.

SAM: Right.

ED: But it could have been a classic.

● ● ● ● ● ● ● ● ●

SAM: Talk about what it was like to play Huey Long.

ED: It was wonderful to play him. I loved doing the script, I loved being down there in the midyear discovering the secrets and the type of support that he had and the fact of his importance to people.

SAM: Did you remember him from when you were a young man?

ED: No, I knew the name, I certainly don't have any information on him, or the fact that his socialism was a threat to Roosevelt. I was particularly told that after we made it, there were problems with presenting it. There was a scene in there in which I am talking to my mistress, who was not openly known as my mistress, but that's what she was. As I lay dying, I say, "Go get yourself a life," or words to that effect. Russell Long was a big finance senator.

SAM: Yeah, Senator Long of Louisiana who was Huey Long's son.

ED: Yeah. And he said, "I don't know what they were trying for." I think he was intimidating NBC is what he was trying. He said, "You gotta do something about that scene. I don't like that scene."

SAM: So, Russell Long killed the scene?

ED: Yeah, he wanted it watered down.

SAM: So, they did.

ED: Watered down and if they hadn't, he would've made certain grants and pluses for NBC.

SAM: He would've made things more difficult.

ED: Difficult, yeah.

SAM: That's interesting.

ED: We filmed in Baton Rouge and one of the places that we ate at and dined at was Jake Staples's restaurant. Jake Staples was a farm boy who Huey saw running chasing rabbits in his farm field and thought he'd be great on the football field, and he created Louisiana State. And Jake Staples, I think, got All-American chasing the rabbits on the field. And he opened his restaurant—he was a nice, old guy. So, we're sitting there one day talking to him, he says, "Yeah, yeah. He was right over there. I saw [whoever the author of the book was, I don't remember] I saw Russell give him a whole bunch of money." Because when I read the book, which was *the* definitive, supposedly definitive book about Huey Long, I said, "When the fuck does he go bad? Where does he go bad?" I mean, he was a prince throughout the whole goddamn book. And when Jake Staples told that story, I said, "Oh, I see."

SAM: So he was saying that Russell paid the biographer to whitewash the story.

ED: Yeah, that was my impression. I don't know if it was true.

SAM: You did a TV movie called *A Small Killing*, 1981 it says. Don't remember it?

ED: I'm trying to.

SAM: It's all right. You've done so many. How about *O'Hara's Wife*.

ED: Yeah. Well what's his name…(William Bartman) was the director…made it with Mariette Hartley and it's a version of *The Ghost and Mrs. Muir*.

SAM: Oh, is that what the story is?

ED: Yeah. It's a good story, and it's funny.

SAM: Jodie Foster was in it when she was young.

ED: Yeah.

SAM: Did you realize she was ever going to be such a big talent at the time?

ED: Oh, she was at the time already.

SAM: Yeah.

ED: Yeah. I think she had already done *Taxi Driver*.

SAM: What was it like working with her?

ED: I can't remember what the role called for, but she did not leave an impression on me. It may have been the role, as I say, which can deaden people, and I've certainly had those roles.

● ● ● ● ● ● ● ● ●

SAM: You were in that movie *Daniel*, that you spoke about the other day. Tell me a little more about it. It was basically about radicals on the run, right?

ED: Based on the E. L. Doctorow book, and Sidney Lumet directing, Tim Hutton was one of the stars.

SAM: He had just won an Oscar, too, right? For *Ordinary People*.

ED: And Lindsay Crouse; she was the mother.

SAM: Who played the father?

ED: Mandy Patinkin. And Julia Bovasso played her mother. Got to go into the room where they were electrocuted. The key moment, for me, was—I'd always seem to shout lines in the crowd scene.

SAM: What part did you play in it?

ED: The lawyer.

SAM: Their lawyer?

ED: Yeah.

SAM: And this is based on the Rosenbergs?

ED: Yeah.

SAM: I thought it was sixties radicals. Okay, Rosenbergs.

ED: So, there's a scene where I'm leaving the kids with the grandmother and either her previous behavior shown or her attitude makes me realize she's going to be fucking it up. And, I give her this speech, you know, "Come on, what is this? Behave. *Vas tustu*." On, on, and on.

SAM: What does that mean? Cause she's not going to be able to know what that meant.

ED: Huh?

SAM: What does the Yiddish that you just said.

ED: *Vas tustu*, what are you doing?

SAM: "What are you doing, what are you doing."

ED: I did it authoritatively, very commandingly. And with that said, "Okay, we got that way now. Now, let's try it totally different. And I did it that way. That's the way it was printed.

SAM: You did it more mellow, yeah.

ED: Very whispery.

SAM: Which one did you like better?

ED: I guess I liked the whispery.

SAM: Okay, so, he made the right choice in your opinion. All right, do you remember a TV movie called *A Case of Libel*?

ED: Of course.

SAM: Who did you play in that?

ED: I played Louis Nizer.

SAM: Oh, you played Louis Nizer, the famous lawyer. Wow.

ED: I don't think that was his name but that's what the play was based on. And, it was Quinton Reynold's suit against Westbrook Pegler.

SAM: Oh, it was based on that.

ED: And a very good Canadian actor (Gordon Pinsent). Dan Travanti played Pegler, and he was brilliant. I had great summation speeches in it and there was a good shout-out against blacklisting.

SAM: So, for people who might not remember Westbrook Pegler, and Quentin Reynolds, who were they? What was the lawsuit about?

ED: Pegler accused of...

SAM: Quentin Reynolds—

ED: Reynolds being a Communist sympathizer. And—

SAM: And Pegler was a well-known columnist, right?

ED: Yeah, rabid. He started as a sports columnist but he became a tremendous influence, politically. He was a viperish, viperish person evidently. So, we nailed him good.

SAM: You played the lawyer for Quentin Reynolds.

ED: Yeah.

SAM: Wow, must have been a fun part.

ED: Mm-hmm.

SAM: Given your politics.

ED: Mm-hmm. You wouldn't have some *schlepper* put in there, would ya?

SAM: No, I wouldn't. It was typecast, in fact. *Anatomy of an Illness*, where you played Norman Cousins.

ED: Cousins, when he came around, he said he would've anticipated a different type of actor portraying him. He thought of himself as on the slim side, not—

SAM: Not heavyset.

ED: But he liked the final product.

SAM: Oh, good, because, you captured him, the essence of him. It must have felt that way.

ED: Mm-hmm.

SAM: That was about how he got through his illness, right?

ED: Mm-hmm.

SAM: He was a sick man; I remember he wrote that famous book. Tell me about *Tender Is the Night*.

ED: Shot that in Switzerland. I thought it was written well, executed well. I guess we didn't break any records.

SAM: It was a TV miniseries.

ED: Mm-hmm.

ED: It was a very esteemed version. Who was the girl?

SAM: Mary Steenburgen and Peter Strauss.

ED: And Peter Strauss?

SAM: Right.

ED: Okay.

SAM: *Tall Tales and Legends.*

ED: What?

SAM: *Tall Tales and Legends.* You don't even remember doing that. TV series. *Vital Signs*, TV movie. Don't remember. *Highway to Heaven.* You had an episode of *Highway to Heaven*.

ED: I played an angel, as usual. I was always fucking up. [*Sam laughs*] and Michael Landon did his best to save me and my fucking up.

SAM: I see.

ED: I was doing good but always tripping at the last moment.

SAM: I see. *The Christmas Star? Kate's Secret?*

ED: Meredith Baxter played a bulimic.

SAM: So, you worked with her again then.

ED: Yeah. And—

SAM: Did you like her?

ED: Yeah. I have a history with her.

SAM: Which was?

ED: She was Jack Fields's step-daughter.

SAM: Oh, so you've known her whole life, pretty much. How long was Jack Fields your agent?

ED: '61 to—I don't remember. Twenty years, at least.

SAM: Mm-hmm. Till the early eighties?

ED: She wasn't crazy about him. Bulimic. And I felt it was a lie because here I was at this weight (heavy).

SAM: So, she wasn't bulimic in real life, but she was bulimic in the show, the movie.

ED: And here I am the weight doctor, psychologist, who's overblown himself.

SAM: So, you felt—

ED: I was miscast.

SAM: Right.

ED: It was their way of making their comment.

SAM: So, I think it was probably more because of your name.

ED: Well, yeah.

SAM: You were Charlie the voice on *Fish Police*. Let's talk for a minute, let's do a talk about that. You've done a lot of voice stuff over the years. Hearing your voice in commercials—

ED: No, you don't.

SAM: Occasionally.

ED: What is it?

SAM: Selling solar panels or something.

ED: Oh, well, shit, one fucking commercial.

SAM: Well, they run it a lot. Anyway, you did a lot of animation voices over the years.

ED: I didn't think so, but I guess when you count it up, it adds.

SAM: We'll get more to that in a minute. *Mattie's Waltz?* Okay, this one you're gonna remember. Guy Bannister in *JFK*. Talk about that.

ED: I was eager to be cast in it thanks to who's directing it.

SAM: Oliver Stone.

ED: Who wrote it?

SAM: Oliver Stone and somebody else. It was based on Jim Garrison's book.

ED: I didn't know anything about Guy Burgess, whatever, yeah Guy Burgess, I think.

SAM: Not Guy Burgess, Guy Bannister. Guy Burgess was the—

ED: English—

SAM: English spy, traitor.

ED: Guy Bannister. Didn't know anything about it, didn't do anything about particular ramifications that took place in New Orleans, in downtown. I got the script to read it and understand it. Started reading it, it was so fucking complex, I said, "Fuck it, I'm not going to try to comprehend this. I'll just stick with Guy Bannister and all that goes on there. And that's what I'll do."

SAM: Yeah, you worked with Jack Lemmon, I remember, in that. Yeah, that was an extraordinary scene. How was working with him?

ED: He was a lovely man.

SAM: Did you know him before that?

ED: Mm-hmm. We were on Broadway together.

SAM: Really? What were you on Broadway with Jack Lemmon in?

ED: It was the first time I was on Broadway.

SAM: *Threepenny Opera?*

ED: No. It was *Face of a Hero* in 1960.

SAM: And did you have fun working with him again after all those years?

ED: Always, yeah. He was a sweet, sweet, wonderful, lovely guy.

SAM: No, okay. So, we're going back to *JFK*, you're with Jack Lemmon. You hadn't worked with him, was that the second time you worked with him since Broadway or the first time since Broadway? And, that was a very interesting relationship because he was sort of very subservient to you. You were very dominant. And, he was sort of a weak, weak person.

ED: Mm-hmm.

SAM: What did you think of the film, *JFK*? Because it was very controversial.

ED: Doesn't matter, because I thought it was beautifully put together.

SAM: Right. What did you think of the premise that it was this conspiracy of these people in New Orleans?

ED: What do I think about it?

SAM: Mm-hmm.

ED: Didn't care about it. There's a book I've read since called *JFK and the Unspeakable*. You know about it?

SAM: No.

ED: Oh, well-addressed book, he was very authoritative, and then he says, "FBI, secret service, and the CIA were all involved in the assassination."

SAM: You know, the one thing that's always seemed clear to me was it wasn't always a lone person.

ED: No.

SAM: That it was a conspiracy. Who was involved, exactly how it happened, a lot of people say it was ridiculous what Stone put forward, but to me, and I remember the day very well—I was in fifth grade when they announced his death—that reading on it and looking at it over the years, if there was more than one shooter, which it seems to be there was, by the very definition then it's a conspiracy.

● ∙ ● ∙ ● ∙ ● ∙ ●

SAM: Tell me about *The Trials of Rosie O'Neill*.

ED: That was a show with my friend Sharon Gless and Tyne Daley. I was still writhing under the cancellation of *Lou Grant* at this point, but the thing that intrigued me overall—forget who I played in it, I don't even know what I played in it—there were a thousand or two thousand people protesting the nonappearance of *Lou Grant* for the summer. And, then finally, they melted away and *Cagney and Lacey* came on. And, they weren't going to be turned into a regular series. There were a thousand people or so, two thousand who protested that. And CBS, this great power and august majesty decided to sign the show up, something they couldn't do with *Lou Grant*.

CBS supported the show strongly at first.
Photo courtesy of CBS

SAM: Who was the exec who was in charge at CBS at the time?

ED: Oh, Paley overwrote everybody.

SAM: So, this was Paley's decision?

ED: Yeah.

SAM: And he was afraid of the Reagan administration.

ED: I guess, yeah.

SAM: So, you say, years later, this is a show, *The Trials of Rosie O'Neill*'s a show with both Sharon Gless and Tyne Daley again? And they also cast you.

ED: Oh, yeah.

SAM: And, you think they brought you in because of what happened years ago?

ED: No. I don't know why they did that. They probably weren't micromanaging that much, but I'm sure, maybe throw them a bone, maybe that'll keep them happy. It's a philosophy that works quite often.

SAM: You did a show called *Freakazoid!* for a few years on and off, do you remember that?

ED: Cartoon show.

SAM: Yeah, cartoon show. Okay, voice, right.

ED: Yeah.

SAM: Okay. What was your favorite—other than *Up*—what was your favorite voice to do in animation?

ED: Granny Good.

SAM: For?

ED: The *Superman* show, I think.

SAM: Oh, okay. You played a woman? Great. You were also on *Mad About You*.

ED: Yeah.

SAM: Small role.

ED: One of my few kinda comedy shows.

SAM: Oh, you were in an episode of *The X-Files*.

ED: Yeah.

SAM: What do you recall about that?

ED: Lily Tomlin was in it with me. What I remember is working late one night, and I'm on one stage, and they had to do a scene with Lily on the adjoining stage. So, they're over there doing it. Finally, they had to stop because there's this noise that keeps coming in, keeps coming in. I was on the next stage snoring.

SAM: Sleeping? [*laughs*] That's very funny.

ED: Couldn't clear me.

SAM: Did you work with Lily herself?

ED: Oh, yeah. It was an interesting segment.

SAM: You worked with David Duchovny and Gillian Armstrong.

ED: She always—it didn't bother me, but she always seemed pissed off.

SAM: Mm-hmm. Okay, you did a bunch of voices. *The Closer*, you were on that show?

ED: That was a Tom Selleck, and David Krumholtz... It was kind of a cute show. Penny Miller was on it, but Les Moonves didn't seem to like it, or he didn't get along well with Tom, so there was no thought of extending it.

SAM: That's interesting, cause Tom Selleck's a big star on a show they have now.

ED: Is that on CBS?

SAM: *Blue Bloods,* yeah.

ED: It's like the old saying, "Kick him off the lot, don't hire him till we need him again."

SAM: Right. *Hard Rain*.

ED: A good movie shot by a foreign director, I forget his name.

SAM: It was with Christian Slater, right?

ED: Yeah.

SAM: And you played a guard, if I remember, right?

ED: Armored car guard.

SAM: Right.

ED: The excessive rain is causing floods and he's working with me, and then we come to a point and we stopped, and they fire at us. Can't do anything about it. I'm in on it, I guess, and I forget what I do. Go back and forth...finally, I think I get winged. I think they come and they take over the whole thing.

SAM: Did you like working with Christian?

ED: Yeah, he's solid.

SAM: *Touched by an Angel*, do you remember that one?

ED: Yeah. They were unhappy with me because I had Bell's palsy at the time, and I tried to sell it as a stroke, but the lady producer was unhappy.

SAM: Do you remember her name?

ED: No.

SAM: I think I had a date with her once. In 2001, you were on *Curb Your Enthusiasm*.

ED: Well, it was one of the first shows. It went well. And I liked what we got, and then as the show went on and on and on and on, I couldn't understand why I wasn't called back to play again. So, finally, I saw Larry David, and I said, "How come you didn't have me back?" He says, "Oh...you died." I replied, "I guess you never watch TV."

SAM: Right. People die and come back on series all the time, particularly if it is running for a long time. So, you had fun on that, anyway. Just looking at different ones here. Mostly voices. *Elf*. Let's talk about *Elf*. You played the classic Santa Claus.

ED: I didn't play a classic Santa Claus.

Three funny guys and me.
Licensed by Warner Bros. Entertainment Inc. All rights reserved

SAM: Oh, okay. Well, to me it was the classic, the best.

ED: Edmund Gwenn is supposedly the classic.

SAM: Well, I thought you were better.

ED: Oh, of course I was. I had balls. And, working with Will Ferrell, you gotta be in top form, or you'll get fucking blown away. So, I had to work my ass off to be that good.

SAM: Did you enjoy it?

ED: I loved Ferrell…wonderful writing, made it suspenseful, casted well. That scene in there where the dwarf wants to beat the shit out of Will Ferrell, oh, priceless scene. So, I had a marvelous two weeks. Jon Favreau directed this classic, whom I adore.

SAM: Great. Then you played Santa Claus again, *The Man Who Saved Christmas*, right? No, you didn't play Santa Claus in that, did you?

ED: I don't think so.

SAM: Yeah. *The Man Who Saved*—that was in 2002. I read somewhere that you played…you've played Santa Claus five times or something?

ED: Oh, at least. Probably eight. I have another one coming out soon.

SAM: 2001, you played Meyer Lansky in *Donzi: The Legend*.

ED: Don-what?

SAM: *Donzi: The Legend* it's called. You played Meyer Lanksy.

ED: I don't remember.

SAM: Oh, okay. It's probably a small part. Do you remember a TV movie in 2005 called *Out of the Woods*?

ED: Sure.

SAM: What was that about?

ED: I'm trying to think of the name of my grandson in it. I can't remember. Jason something (Jason London). And, it's about an eccentric who, I guess, has amassed money over his lifetime, and is prepared for the wind as he thinks he has to be subjected to it over the weekend.

SAM: He's going to die, he thinks.

ED: Yeah.

SAM: Right.

ED: Cause the acting is strong, but they can't go anywhere unless following that script, which is what we did.

SAM: All right, here's the big one. *Up.*

ED: Yeah.

SAM: Of all the films you ever done, I think that one has resonated more with people than anyone I know, that you've done. I mean people—obviously *The Mary Tyler Moore* and *Lou Grant* were ongoing things, but as a single project, *Up* really moves people.

ED: Yeah. You're right. It is a beautiful movie. And, how I refer to it, it's like a double love story.

SAM: Mm-hmm.

ED: First Ellie, and then slowly but surely, by the end of the film, the kid, with a few appendages.

● ● ● ● ● ● ● ● ● ● ●

SAM: You know, I remember you in an episode of *Arliss* about the sport's agent played by Robert Wuhl where you played a baseball TV announcer that they wanted to fire.

ED: And it was kind of like a guy with a reputation of—

SAM: Vin Sculley.

ED: Vin Sculley.

SAM: Yeah. And I remember you had this expression of, "Hey, hey, what do ya say?" And I remember that. And it was very moving because you make an announcement…talk about that role.

ED: I don't remember anything about it.

SAM: You don't remember anything about it, okay.

ED: What did you start to say?

SAM: I was so moved by that performance.

ED: Yeah, but I start to make an announcement, and what?

SAM: You tell the whole world that you have Alzheimer's disease.

ED: Oh, I do?

SAM: Yeah, cause you're losing it during the episode—the guy who bought the team wants to fire you, but everybody else wants to keep you and then you realize that you have to—that it's time to go, that you can't really do it anymore. But, you're aware enough to make the announcement to the whole world. It's extraordinarily a moving scene.

ED: Thank you.

SAM: *Too Big to Fail.* I remember liking this film very much. You played Warren Buffet.

ED: Yeah.

SAM: In 2011. What do you remember about that? Basically, it was a phone call. That was the whole scene.

ED: I got to play it with kids. Kids were nice. And he was there to watch it.

SAM: Warren Buffet? Did you get to meet him?

ED: Mm-hmm. And he liked it a lot. He was tremendously buoyed.

SAM: Oh, that's wonderful. Did you ask him any financial advice? [*laughs*]

ED: I would not have understood it.

SAM: *Hot in Cleveland* with Betty White.

ED: Yeah.

SAM: Did you play a suitor?

ED: That was another disappointment. I didn't really have anything to do, and I guess my ego took over. Questioning, why are you there? Why are you there?

SAM: If you were going to be there, you wanted to have more of a role.

ED: I mean, nothing against Betty, of course, 'cause she's the greatest in the world, but, it's—

SAM: You deserved a richer part, you feel.

● ● ● ● ● ● ● ● ●

SAM: And let's continue onward, a bunch of other series. I saw in this, on *Criminal Minds*, you played the father of one of the characters, right?

ED: Father-in-law.

SAM: Father-in-law. It was a very moving performance; I was really touched by it.

ED: Really?

SAM: Your character was very bitter at him because you felt he was responsible for his daughter's death. Talk about doing that part.

ED: Well, thing of being a part of that family—that show's off the air now, right?

SAM: I don't think so. Well, have reruns all the time. I think it's still running.

ED: Oh, well, he's (Thomas Gibson) off?

SAM: I think he's off, yeah.

ED: That's a shame. Glad Joe Mantegna is still on it though. He and I have crossed paths with autism causes—good guy! You didn't see my *Good Wife*, did you?

SAM: No, talk about that. I might've missed that.

ED: I played someone who's helping her in her campaign. And I'm filled with homophobic sentiments every time I open my mouth. [*Sam laughs*] It was great to play such a piece of ungodly shit.

SAM: You enjoyed it, huh? Let's talk about Franklin Roosevelt. You got to play that wonderful part in a one-man show that I saw. It was extraordinary. It was the first time you met my wife, you know? We went backstage, and you know the first thing you said to her? "Come sit on my lap."

ED: What's wrong with that?

SAM: Nothing. She didn't do it though.

ED: And she still hasn't.

SAM: She deserves you, I know. Go ahead. Talk about FDR.

ED: He was a god when I was growing up. Still is a god. It's was very fortunate, greatness chose him.

SAM: He was the right man, at the right time. So it was a joy and an honor for you to play him, wasn't it?

ED: Mm-hmm.

SAM: That was a lot of lines to learn! That was like an hour and a half, two-hour show, just you. Have you always had—

ED: I won't make that mistake again.

SAM: Have you always had a good memory?

ED: Yeah.

SAM: Has it been hard for you to memorize lines over the years?

ED: Not really. I'm not trying now.

SAM: I understand. But I mean, back in the day. You could do it pretty easily?

ED: When you surrender yourself to someone that includes letting the brain flow to the words.

SAM: What is the most important thing about being an actor to you? Other than the fame, or money, whatever. What's the most important thing as a human being, in your soul, that acting has afforded you, or allowed you to do?

ED: There have been periodic times, when, as an actor, what I have done affected people, taught people, and gratified people. And when they have gone through the obstacles so they could get up next to me, and either write me or tell me that you did such and such, and you affected me this way, it tends to make you feel like a god. And, you've had one of those occasional touches of power.

SAM: You know what it is for me? That those moments, that truth that you've actually affected millions of people, says to me your life has mattered—it matters.

ED: Well, sure, yeah. I know my life matters. And then after the realization streaks across my brain, *What the fuck am I doing here?*

SAM: With me!

ED: With you, yeah. Why am I being wasted now?

SAM: One word: ageism.

ED: People who know, know that they can reach down and pluck me up, and put me here at the right moment. And I'd look and say—

SAM: And deliver.

ED: Time and time again. I just did a film in Canada. Lots of good actors. I'm very surprised how—I seemed flawless. I'll rarely say that about myself. But I was never embarrassed. And, there's so much more to be there to have fun with. Take advantage of it.

● ● ● ● ● ● ● ● ● ● ●

SAM: And how about the philosophy of being an activist?

ED: Do the right thing. Being an activist probably means you have to say, correct the wrong thing. And there are a lot of wrong things. So it's a good thing that we were confronted with choices, and I think the hardest thing for me is to have two equal choices and not be able to support both.

SAM: Well, as far as I'm concerned, in total, looking back in all these years, you've definitely done the right thing.

ED: Yeah. I don't know.

● ● ● ● ● ● ● ● ● ● ●

SAM: Any last thoughts?

ED: I look at my father and my mother, and what good people they were. My sisters, brothers, who were good people. Strong people. They're lying, molding in a fucking grave. They're worms by now, ashes. Whatever they are. I'm thinking that that's what they came to and where's their legacy? Where's their honor? Where are their Emmys? Why the fuck do we even bother? Who cares?

SAM: You know, Ed, if you didn't care, you wouldn't still be advocating for causes and fighting for what you believe in.

ED: No, I know, I know. Some of those causes because I've already been pledged to them. I don't want to back away from them.

SAM: But that's still an ethic.

ED: Yeah. What a shame that they're dead and I never did give them as much as I would have liked to, my kids, too. It takes energy. You know, I have only so much energy. So, I'm sorry I didn't give them more energy. All of them.

SAM: Well, you've given the world a lot of joy, and I love you, Ed.

ACKNOWLEDGEMENTS

For years, people have asked me, "Why don't you write an autobiography? You have a story that people would love to hear!" I simply ignored them. I know that I've had a long career. Heck, I am eighty-eight and still acting!

It wasn't until my last sibling, Labe, passed away a little over a year ago that I realized it was time.

I have all these memories of my family. Every once in a while a story will pop into my head out of nowhere and I will think of them. Memories stay with us.

I wrote this book so that my family can read it when I am gone and hopefully smile while remembering a story about me.

This book is not just a story about Hollywood or celebrities, but about a West Bottoms Jew, who worked in a junkyard and defied all odds to be where he is today.

I want to thank many people, some for helping with this book and others for being a part of my life and creating these memories with me.

My parents, Morris and Lizzie, for believing in their little boy and providing him with endless opportunities in life. Who'd think that the owners

I admired my brother very much.
Courtesy of Asner Family Photo Collection

of a junkyard could provide so much for a house filled with five children? That's the power of love for ya.

My brothers, Ben and Labe, for being my inspirations for Lou Grant. Without their jabs, taunts, and overall devilish nature, they might have cast Mickey Rooney to play Lou. Who knows where I'd be then?

My sisters, Esther and Eve, for always taking care of their baby brother. They happily changed my diapers when I was a child. Now, if only they were still around to change them today…

My four children, Matt, Liza, Katie, and Charlie, whom I consider to be my greatest life achievements. My Emmys have got nothing on these beautiful and smart kids. I only wish they could fit in my awards cabinet…

I adored my big sister.
Courtesy of Asner Family Photo Collection

My grandchildren, each one of you has a spark of greatness like this world has never seen before. Show them who you truly are. Be yourselves and never forget where you come from. And, as a side note, just know that baldness skips a generation. Please apologize to your hairlines on my behalf.

Cindy Asner, for making Charles Asner possible.

George Corporon, for teaching me the possibilities in this world concerning news, and Ed Ellis, my beloved football coach, for teaching me the meaning of tough, but fair.

Nick Granado, for being the only man who can appreciate a good steak at lunchtime…when someone else is picking up the tab.

Chris Ostman, Jack McMahon, Zach Lyons, and Michael Manoukian, for unknowingly volunteering to provide sponge baths in exchange for credit in this book.

Joseph and Sally Wilson, for guidance, motivation, and teaching us all the fine art of eating food from a can. Who doesn't love deviled ham in a can?!

T. Barrett Curtin, for his support, generosity, and paying it forward. A true gent, even though he is a Boston Red Sox fan.

Gary and Patricia Seymour, for always offering a helping hand. A great couple, who single-handedly keeps the jumpsuit industry in business.

Steve and Sonja Sher, for their encouragement, believing in the authors of this book, and providing a good fart joke when a laugh was needed.

Margaret Shields, a remarkable woman with a heart of gold. She survived the war only to endure the agony of reading this book.

Alejandra (Mier) Seymour, whose encouragement during the creation of this book inspired the authors to complete the difficult task of actually writing a book. If not for her marriage to one of the authors, and the fact that English is her second language, she would probably receive an editor's credit.

And special thanks to my beautiful, talented daughter Liza and the final editing she did of the manuscript and the incredible effort she made in finding and organizing the photographs.

Last, but certainly not least, my Nancy, you are and always will be my everything. We shared thirty years of our lives together. Thank you for loving me, putting up with me, and seeing potential in me. This schlub didn't deserve you in his life. Luckily, you disagreed. Thank you.

Finally, I dedicate this book to all of you in the West Bottoms. Kansas City is my home. Even though I moved to California, I will always be a West Bottom Jew in my heart.

Mazel tov!

NOTES

Introduction

[1] *"a person who deals in resalable junk."*: Merriam-Webster. "Junkman | Definition of Junkman by Merriam-Webster." Accessed July 26, 2018. https://www.merriam-webster.com/dictionary/junkman.
[2] *"something of poor quality"*: Merriam-Webster. "Junk | Definition of Junkman by Merriam-Webster." Accessed July 26, 2018. https://www.merriam-webster.com/dictionary/junk.
[3] *"something of little meaning, worth, or significance "*: Ibid.
[4] *"old iron, glass, paper, or other waste that may be used again in some form"*: Ibid.
[5] *"secondhand, worn, or discarded articles"*: Ibid.

Chapter 9: Oh, Mr. Grant

[1] *"Hannibal Lecter with an intense appetite for Jodie Foster's liver"*: Moore, Mary Tyler, *After All* (New York: G.P. Putnam's Sons, 1995), p. 151.

Chapter 11: "The Jane Fonda of Latin America"

[1] SAG-AFTRA. "Edward Asner 1981–1985." Accessed July 26, 2018. https://www.sagaftra.org/edward-asner.

Samuel Warren Joseph has been a professional writer for more than 40 years. His credits include the feature films *Off Your Rocker* and *Window of Opportunity*. His animation credits include shows like *Duck Tales*, *Dennis the Menace*, and *Batman: The Animated Series*. His produced stage plays include *Moral Imperative* and *Two Times Two*, and two musicals: *Campaign* and *Psychosexual: A Love Story*. Most recently he co-wrote *God Help Us!*- which stars Ed Asner as God moderating a political debate and is playing around the country. Sam is also an adjunct professor of English and lives in southern California with his beautiful wife, Sandra.

Matthew Seymour is a writer and practicing attorney from Turlock, California. He obtained his law degree from Santa Clara University School of Law and his bachelor's degree in history from the University of California, Santa Barbara. Mr. Seymour has contributed to numerous articles featured in national media outlets including *The Huffington Post* and *Law360*. He previously collaborated with Mr. Asner on his book *The Grouchy Historian*. Mr. Seymour and his wife currently reside in Orange County, California.